XML and SQL

XML and SQL

Developing Web Applications

Daniel K. Appelquist

▲▼Addison-Wesley

Boston • San Francisco • New York • Toronto • Montreal
London • Munich • Paris • Madrid
Capetown • Sydney • Tokyo • Singapore • Mexico City

Many of the designations used by manufacturers and sellers to distinguish their products are claimed as trademarks. Where those designations appear in this book, and Addison-Wesley was aware of a trademark claim, the designations have been printed with initial capital letters or in all capitals.

The author and publisher have taken care in the preparation of this book, but make no expressed or implied warranty of any kind and assume no responsibility for errors or omissions. No liability is assumed for incidental or consequential damages in connection with or arising out of the use of the information or programs contained herein.

The publisher offers discounts on this book when ordered in quantity for special sales. For more information, please contact:

Pearson Education Corporate Sales Division
201 W. 103rd Street
Indianapolis, IN 46290
(800) 428-5331
corpsales@pearsoned.com

Visit AW on the Web: www.aw.com/cseng/

Library of Congress Control Number: 2001 135206

Copyright © 2002 Pearson Education, Inc

All rights reserved. No part of this publication may be reproduced, stored in a retrieval system, or transmitted, in any form, or by any means, electronic, mechanical, photocopying, recording, or otherwise, without the prior consent of the publisher. Printed in the United States of America. Published simultaneously in Canada.

For information on obtaining permission for use of material from this work, please submit a written request to:

Pearson Education, Inc.
Rights and Contracts Department
75 Arlington Street, Suite 300
Boston, MA 02116
Fax: (617) 848-7047

ISBN 0-201-65796-1
Text printed on recycled paper
1 2 3 4 5 6 7 8 9 10—MA—0504030201
First printing, December 2001

For Allison and Alexander

Contents

Introduction xiii
   Who Should Read This Book? xiii
   Why Would You Read This Book? xiv
   The Structure of This Book xv
   My Day Job in the Multimodal World xvi

Acknowledgments xxi

About the Author xxiii

Chapter 1   **Why XML?** 1
   The Lesson of SGML 1
   What About XML? 3
   Why HTML Is Not the Answer 3
   The Basics of XML 5
   Why You Don't Need to Throw Away Your RDBMS 7
   A Brief Example 8
   Great! How Do I Get Started? 9
   Summary 10

Chapter 2	**Introducing XML and SQL: A History Lesson of Sorts**	**11**
	Extensible Markup Language (XML)	12
	Evaluating XML's Design Goals	*14*
	Structured Query Language (SQL)	18
	What Is "Relational"?	*19*
	Fitting It All Together	22
	Summary	24
Chapter 3	**Project Definition and Management**	**25**
	An Illustrative Anecdote	25
	How to Capture Requirements	27
	CyberCinema: The Adventure Begins	29
	Requirements Gathering	30
	User Scenarios	*30*
	Functional Requirements Document	35
	Quality Assurance	38
	Unit Testing	*39*
	Integration Testing	*39*
	Project Management	42
	Dynamic Systems Development Method (DSDM)	*42*
	Extreme Programming!	*43*
	The Technical Specification Document	45
	Summary	46
Chapter 4	**Data Modeling**	**49**
	Getting Data-Centric	50
	Show Me the Data!	*52*
	What Do You Hope to Accomplish?	*53*

Making It Visual: Entity Relationship Diagrams *54*
Roll Film: Back to CyberCinema *54*
Normalization Equals Power: Defining Relationships *56*
Keep It Simple: No Really, I Mean It *56*
Getting Complex: Many-to-One and Many-to-Many Relationships *58*
Another Layer of Complexity: Adding Media *59*
Summary 61

Chapter 5   XML Design **63**
Carving Your Rosetta Stone 64
When to Use XML and When Not to Use It 66
Think Like an Archeologist *66*
Building a DTD 68
CyberCinema: The Rosetta Stone Meets the Web 72
The Head *74*
The Body *79*
Building XML DTDs: Let the Experts Do Hard Stuff 85
Summary 86

Chapter 6   Getting Relational: Database Schema Design . . **89**
Knowing When to Let Go 90
First Steps 91
SQL and XML: The Joys of Partial Decomposition *94*
Decomposing CyberCinema 100
XML Nitro Injection: Adding Reviews 104
Link Management 105
Selecting What You Need 108
Using Link Management to Help Power Suggestions 109
Summary 113

Chapter 7 Related Standards: XSLT, XML Schema, and Other Flora and Fauna 115

XSLT: XML Transformers! 116
So How Does XSLT Work Exactly? 118
XML Schema: An Alternative to DTDs 121
Querying XML Documents 126
XML Query 126
SQLX: The Truth Is Out There 127
Summary 128

Chapter 8 XML and SQL Server 2000 129

Retrieving Data in XML Format 130
FOR XML 131
FOR XML AUTO 132
FOR XML EXPLICIT 133
Communicating with SQL Server over the Web 134
Under the Hood 135
Retrieving Data in XML Format—Continued 136
SQL Queries in URLs 137
Template Files 138
XPath Queries 141
HTTP Post Queries 141
XML Views 141
Defining XML Views 144
Let SQL Server Do the Work 146
Working with XML Documents 152
OPENXML 152
Summary 155

Chapter 9 Java Programming with XML and SQL 157

Dealing with XML in Java 159

Building Java Objects for XML Instances with DOM *161*
Using SAX Events to Drive XML Partial Decomposition *163*
Invoking XSLT Transformations *165*
Designing an Entity Bean for Movie Reviews *166*
To Transform or Not to Transform *171*
JDBC, JNDI, and EJBs *172*
JNDI *173*
Bean Persistence *174*
JDBC Advanced Data Types *174*
On the Near Horizon: XML Data Binding *175*
J2EE Application Servers *175*
Summary *176*

Chapter 10 More Examples: Beyond Silly Web Sites 179

Building a Web Service *180*
Corporate Phone Directory *180*
Stock Quotes *181*
E-Commerce *185*
Taxonomical Structure *188*
Document Management and Content Locking *192*
Versioning and Change Management *195*
Summary *197*

Appendix 201

Bibliography 209

Index 211

Introduction

This book is about how you can use Extensible Markup Language (XML) and relational databases in the real world to solve real problems (as opposed to the sometimes academic world of standards bodies and other groups that promote standards usage). In other words, you can really *use* XML—it's not just hype. In this book, you will find concrete examples, insight into the application development life cycle as I've known it, and a discussion of the why, the how, and the where of building applications (with a special focus on Web applications) using the tools of XML and relational databases.

This book is not intended to be a comprehensive guide. It's an overview of the field, packed with good ideas and witty commentary, which should get you started in the right direction. The areas I've focused the most attention on are ones in which I have something useful to say. In other areas, I've provided an overview of concepts, and, instead of reinventing the wheel, I've included URLs that point you to useful and informative Web resources.

Who Should Read This Book?

This book is intended primarily for software developers who are managing small- to medium-scale projects. My experience is mostly from working on small development teams, where resource limitations often dictate that the person writing the requirements for a project is also the engineer in charge of design and coding. This book is written from that perspective.[1] If you work in a larger, more structured team or environment, you may find it strange that I'm talking about requirements gathering in one sentence and data modeling in the next, but this book can also be useful to you, if applied correctly. I've organized the chapters into the different stages of application design so that you can read through the entire book or flip to a particular piece of interest. In either case, you'll come away with something useful.

Familiarity with the concepts of databases and markup languages (specifically, knowledge of HyperText Markup Language—HTML) will make this book easier to understand. If you're new to markup languages and SQL, you'll still find this book helpful in explaining how they can be used together to develop applications. In addition, I recommend you read *XML: A Manager's Guide* by Kevin Dick (1999) for an overview of the XML language and its features. I also recommend *SQL Queries for Mere Mortals: A Hands-On Guide to Data Manipulation in SQL* by Michael J. Hernandez (2000).

Why Would You Read This Book?

Good question! I started writing this book after I worked on a content management application at TheStreet.com, which is an online financial news service—essentially an electronic newspaper—complete with journalists, editors, reporters, contributors, and columnists. TheStreet.com's publishing model was "multichannel"; they published their articles to their Web site (one "channel" of publication). They also published to other channels, such as syndicating articles to other sites (Microsoft Network, Yahoo!, and so forth) and to devices (PDAs, cell phones, pagers, what-have-you). This book is a result of my experiences in building a content management strategy for TheStreet.com and an application of everything I learned during that time, combined with in-depth material that I've picked up along the way. This book is best read when you're starting work on a project that has a content management component and you're thinking of using XML and a SQL database.

[1.] A word on humor: In this book, I use humor because it's my way of expressing myself. My apologies to anyone who doesn't find me funny; nonetheless, I hope you find the information in this book useful and are able to read between my tired japes.

The Structure of This Book

This book is broken into ten chapters, corresponding roughly to the stages of application design and development.

1. **Why XML?**   Notice I'm not asking the more mundane question, "What is XML?" This chapter instead delves into some specific examples of why XML is useful and why you want to start building systems with it.
2. **Introducing XML and SQL: A History Lesson of Sorts.**   Chapter 2 provides a brief description of XML, its history and structure, and what it brings to the table. A similar discussion of SQL and the rise of the relational database follows.
3. **Project Definition and Management.**   This chapter is a primer on getting the requirements for your system down on paper. It's included because I think this step is important, and I've often seen it done badly. Chapter 3 also discusses thinking about requirements from a perspective of building a "data-oriented" application. This chapter introduces two examples: a simple e-mail application and the CyberCinema Web site.
4. **Data Modeling.**   After you have gathered your requirements, you have to start thinking abstractly about your data. It's a tough world out there, and without a bullet-proof data model to protect you, you're going to wake up one day and realize your life has been a dismal failure.
5. **XML Design.**   You know why you should use XML because you read Chapter 1, but do you know where you should use it? What parts of your data make sense for XML, and what parts should remain purely relational? This chapter discusses the design of your XML documents, focusing on the document type definition (DTD) as a vehicle for this discussion.
6. **Getting Relational: Database Schema Design.**   Now that you have your data model and your XML design, how do you best write a data schema to get the job done? This chapter is brimming with helpful examples.

7. **Related Standards: XSLT, XML Schema, XML Query, and Other Flora and Fauna.** What do you do with all this XML once you have it? This is where the Extensible Stylesheet Language (XSL) comes into play. XSL can be used to translate XML for display or internal purposes. It can also be leveraged to aid in partial decomposition. XML Schema provides an alternative to DTDs in defining XML document structure. Query languages on the near horizon promise to query XML documents and SQL databases.
8. **XML and SQL Server 2000.** So how do you take all this XML and relational data and turn it into a real, living, breathing *application*—one that's actually useful and *works*? Here's one answer: Use the comprehensive XML support found in Microsoft's SQL Server 2000. This chapter presents a discussion of those features and delves into how you might use them to implement some of the strategies previously discussed.
9. **Java Programming with XML and SQL.** Another implementation strategy for your XML applications is to build them using the J2EE (Java 2 Enterprise Edition) framework. Chapter 9 introduces this framework and discusses some of its XML-specific features.
10. **More Examples: Beyond Silly Web Sites.** Chapter 10 provides other concrete examples of how to mix XML and SQL harmoniously.

My Day Job in the Multimodal World

Since I started writing this book, I've actually moved on from leading development teams. My most recent work has been on a more conceptual level, and some of the chapters of this book, particularly Chapter 3, which deals with requirements gathering, draw from this work.

My latest work is on something I call the "multimodal" world, a world in which consumers interact seamlessly with services through the most convenient devices or modalities at hand. The breakneck speed with which the e-revolution has engulfed us has left the world in a shambles, leaving consumers feeling helpless and frustrated. I've been looking back with a little bit of pragmatism and figuring out what we've really accomplished. People, who today have the tools of technology, have unprecedented access to information, products, and services, but they still don't have seamless access to the information they need. The popularity of the Net has forced everyone to become part-time computer support technicians. The advent of wireless and Internet devices and digital television has brought these technologies closer to becoming "appliances," a ubiquitous and seamlessly integrated part of people's lives. But people have a much different expectation of appliances than they do of the Internet. Internet browsers are allowed to crash; microwave ovens can't. Appliances have to work reliably and integrate themselves into our daily lives—seamlessly.

Let me give you an example of how technology hasn't interacted seamlessly with my life. Recently I was waiting for a replacement American Express credit card to arrive in the mail. I called customer service at American Express several times and was assured that the card was on its way. Finally I received a letter from SDS (Special Delivery Services, a company I had no previous dealings with or knowledge of), informing me that they had tried to deliver a new American Express card, but nobody had been home. The letter listed a Web address, an e-mail address, and a phone number for me to use to arrange delivery. The form I filled out on the SDS Web site yielded a system error. I tried the e-mail option with no results. Finally I called the number and was placed on eternal hold.

The interjection of the unknown company, SDS, shatters the seamless integration of my experience as an American Express customer. SDS's lack of customer service isn't American Express's fault, but I'm still left with a bad taste in my mouth. Likewise American Express's "handoff" to SDS means that their customer service staff and information systems are unaware of the disposition of my replacement card. Unfortunately this sort of thing happens all the time, and the results are not always as innocuous as my charge card replacement problem.

Here's an example of how this scenario might play out in a world where consumers interact more seamlessly with technology (the multimodal world). When I discovered that my card was lost, I could have registered this information using my Internet-enabled mobile phone. A customer service agent would have called me to arrange for delivery. If I wasn't at home to receive the package, I could have received a message on my mobile phone, directing me to an interactive service or a Web page on which I could arrange for redelivery.

Or I could have called my American Express customer service agent to arrange delivery, or perhaps they would call *me* (imagine that!).

This example implies a tight integration between American Express and its delivery company and an ability for consistent information to flow between different systems within American Express—their Web site, their customer service systems, their Wireless Application Protocol (WAP) systems, and so forth. That kind of integration, in turn, implies standard languages and protocols with which businesses can communicate with other businesses as well as with consumers. XML facilitates this layer of standardization by providing a framework on which to base those standard languages. For instance, American Express might use a specialized XML-based business-to-business (B2B) language to communicate with suppliers. XML is the glue that can make this kind of integration possible—both inside and outside an enterprise—which is why I'm passionate about XML becoming even more pervasive than it is today.

Another enabler of this world of seamless interaction is content management. In the multimodal world, consumers should be able to use whatever device is most conveniently at hand to accomplish their goal—make transactions, find information, send or receive messages, whatever. If I want to check the weather report for tomorrow or book a flight from New York to Hong Kong, I should be able to use any device, for example, a mobile phone. When obtaining weather information, I may want it spoken to me while I'm in a car, but I'll want to read it on the screen when I'm in a meeting. A mobile phone might be sufficient to determine weather conditions. For flight information, I might want to stop the transaction once I hear some of the initial fares and finish when I'm in front of a Web browser, or I might want to call a customer service agent who is aware of my fare search and preferences. This kind of consistent and seamless access to information in different formats implies robust content management, and XML is a key enabling technology for content management. XML also plays a role in the delivery of information and applications to different platforms because the languages these devices speak (such as WML and xHTML) are built on top of XML.

An "emergent property" of a system is a property or capability that "emerges" only after the pieces are put together in the right way. If you mix a bunch of proteins with water in a bowl, you wouldn't expect them to start reciting from Shakespeare's *Hamlet, Prince of Denmark,* but the human brain, which is essentially a mass of neatly arranged proteins, has emergent properties of intelligence, self-awareness, and creativity. The proliferation of Internet-connected devices and the widespread adoption of XML and XML-linked technologies in B2B, B2C (business-to-consumer), and B2E (business-to-employee) communications and transactions will develop an emergent property: the radical transformation of global business. As astounding as the rise of the Internet and the industry shift toward e-enabled services have been over the past five years, it is nothing compared with the transformation of business that is to come.

Acknowledgments

This book is the result of my experience in building Internet applications. Because most of these projects were collaborative, everyone I've worked with since 1995 is owed some measure of gratitude and has, in some way, contributed to this work.

I'd like to thank Dan Woods, who suggested that I write a book and introduced me to the fine people at Addison-Wesley. I didn't know what I was getting myself into at the time, but thanks nonetheless. I'd like to thank all the staff at Addison-Wesley, Alicia Carey, Jacquelyn Doucette, and especially Mary O'Brien for being patient with me throughout this process. I'd also like to thank Nancy Crumpton, who worked as a developmental editor on this project and helped immeasurably in making this material more useful, curbing my more egregious stylistic tendencies.

I'd like to thank all my reviewers: Keith W. Hare, Michael J. Hernandez, Robert W. Husted, Tim Kientzle, Leo Korman, J.J. Kuslich (who went on to contribute much of the information regarding SQL Server 2000), Edward Piou, Naohiko Uramoto, and John L. Viescas. Your comments and attention to detail helped me make this book better and more complete.

The idea for this book originated with the work I was doing at TheStreet.com, and as such I'd like to thank my colleagues who worked with me in various capacities on that project: Gerald Adams, Scott Cohen, Martin Coughlan, Eric Gilmore, Amr Halem, Federico Hattoum, Alan O'Regan, Robert Sorkin, Rens Troost, and Evan Turtel. Together, we gave a new meaning to the word "Rosebud."

Going back a bit further, I'd like to thank Rich Wiklund, who gave me the opportunity to learn everything I know about XML and SQL and about building Internet applications.

Finally, I owe a debt of gratitude to my amazing wife Allison, who put up with my moodiness throughout this project, even though I moved us from Washington to New York and then to London over the course of four years. Our next project will be a joint one.

About the Author

Daniel Appelquist has more than eleven years of experience in the Internet services industry. In 1989, he founded an online fiction magazine, *Quanta*, which published for five years. He has a Bachelor of Science degree in Cognitive Science from Carnegie Mellon University. In 1995 he helped to create E-Doc, a company that provided Web development services to the scientific, technical, and medical publishing industry. Working with publishers such as John Wiley & Sons and Macmillan Press, he was the architect of the SGML-based publishing systems behind the online editions of the journals *Cancer*, *Nature*, and many others. At TheStreet.com, he was the architect of their XML-based publishing system. Subsequently, he filled the role of CTO for TheStreet.co.uk was vice president of Global Technology for TheStreet.com. Subsequently, as a consultant, he worked on many European e-business projects. Dan has also worked at AOL's Digital City, New Century Network, and the consulting firm Codefab. He has spoken at numerous trade shows and events, including Seybold and XTech, has been active on the advisory committee of the W3C and in the Open Group's Mobile Management Forum, has served as an advisory member of the ICE protocol group, and is on the advisory board of Kinecta Corporation.

He currently lives in London and is an independent consultant, specializing in content management and e-business strategy.

Chapter 1

Why XML?

> In which it is revealed where my personal experience of markup languages began.

In this chapter, I take you through some of my initial experiences with markup languages, experiences that led me to be such an advocate of information standards in general and markup languages in particular. We discuss a simple example of the power of markup, and throughout the chapter, I cover some basic definitions and concepts.

The Lesson of SGML

In early 1995, I helped start a company, E-Doc, with a subversive business plan based on the premise that big publishing companies (in this case, in the scientific-technical-medical arena) might want to publish on the World Wide Web. I say "subversive" because at the time it was just that—the very companies we were targeting with our services were the old guard of the publishing world, and they had every reason in the world to suppress and reject these new technologies. A revolution was already occurring, especially in the world of scientific publishing. Through the Internet, scientists were beginning to share papers with other scientists. While the publishing companies weren't embracing this new medium, the scientists themselves were, and in the process they were bypassing traditional journal publication entirely and threatening decades of entrenched academic practice. Remember, the Internet wasn't seen as a viable commercial medium back then; it was largely used by academics, although we were starting to hear about the so-called "information superhighway." Despite the assurance of all my friends that I was off my rocker, I left my secure career in the client/server software industry to follow my nose into the unknown. In my two years at E-Doc, I learned a great deal about technology, media, business, and the publishing industry, but one lesson that stands out is the power of SGML.

An international standard since 1986, SGML (Standard Generalized Markup Language) is the foundation on which modern markup languages (such as HTML or Hypertext Markup Language, the language of the Web) are based. SGML defines a structure through which markup languages can be built. HTML is a flavor of SGML, but it is only one markup language (and not even a particularly complex one) that derives from SGML. Since its inception, SGML has been in use in publishing, as well as in industry and governments throughout the world.

Because many of the companies we were dealing with at E-Doc had been using flavors of SGML to encode material such as books and journal articles since the late 1980s, they had developed vast storehouses of SGML data that was just waiting for the Internet revolution. Setting up full-text Web publishing systems became a matter of simply translating these already existing SGML files. It's not that the decision makers at these companies were so forward-thinking that they knew a global network that would redefine the way we think about information would soon develop. The lesson of SGML was precisely that these decision makers did not know what the future would hold. Using SGML "future-proofed" their data so that when the Web came around, they could easily repurpose it for their changing needs.

It's been a wild ride over the past six years, but as we begin a new century and a new millennium, that idea of future-proofing data seems more potent and relevant than ever. The publishing industry will continue to transform and accelerate into new areas, new platforms, and new paradigms. As technology professionals, we have to start thinking about future-proofing now, while we're still at the beginning of this revolution.

What About XML?

So what do SGML and the Internet revolution have to do with XML? Let me tell you a secret: XML is just SGML wearing a funny hat; XML is SGML with a sexy name. In other words, XML is an evolution of SGML. The problem with SGML is that it takes an information management professional to understand it. XML represents an attempt to simplify SGML to a level where it can be used widely. The result is a simplified version of SGML that contains all the pieces of SGML that people were using anyway. Therefore, XML can help anyone future-proof content against future uses, whatever those might be.

That's power, baby!

Why HTML Is Not the Answer

I hear you saying to yourself, "Ah, Dan, but what about HTML? I can use HTML for managing information, and I get Web publishing for free (because HTML is the language of the Web). Isn't HTML also derived from SGML, and isn't it also a great, standardized way of storing documents?" Well, yes on one, no on two. HTML is wonderful, but for all its beauty, HTML is really good only at describing layout—it's a display-oriented markup. Using HTML, you can make a word **bold** or *italic*, but as to the reason that word might be bold or italic, HTML remains mute. With XML, because you define the markup you want to use in your documents, you can mark a certain word as a person's name or the title of a book. When the document is *represented*, the word will appear bold or italic; but with XML, because your documents know all the locations of people's names or book titles, you can capriciously decide that you want to underline book titles across the board. You have to make this change only once, wherever your XML documents are being represented. And that's just the beginning. Your documents are magically transformed from a bunch of relatively dumb HTML files to documents with intelligence, documents with muscle.

If I hadn't already learned this lesson, I learned it again when migrating TheStreet.com (the online financial news service that I referred to in the Introduction) from a relatively dumb HTML-based publishing system to a relatively smart XML-based content management system. When I joined TheStreet.com, it had been running for over two years with archived content (articles) that needed to be migrated to the new system. This mass of content was stored only as HTML files on disk. A certain company (which shall remain nameless) had built the old system, apparently assuming that no one would ever have to do anything with this data in the future besides spit it out in exactly the same format. With a lot of Perl (then the lingua franca of programming languages for the Web and an excellent tool for writing data translation scripts) and one developer's hard-working and largely unrecognized efforts over the course of six months, we managed to get most of it converted to XML. Would it have been easier to start with a content management system built from the ground up for repurposing content? Undoubtedly!

If this tale doesn't motivate you sufficiently, consider the problem of the wireless applications market. Currently, wireless devices (such as mobile phones, Research In Motion's Blackberry pager, and the Palm VII wireless personal digital assistant) are springing up all over, and content providers are hot to trot out their content onto these devices. Each of these devices implements different markup languages. Many wireless devices use WML (Wireless Markup Language, the markup language component of WAP, Wireless Application Protocol), which is built on top of XML. Any content providers who are already working with XML are uniquely positioned to get their content onto these devices. Anyone who isn't is going to be left holding the bag.

So HTML or WML or whatever you like becomes an output format (the display-oriented markup) for our XML documents. In building a Web publishing system, display-oriented markup happens at the representation stage, the very last stage. When our XML document is represented, it is represented in HTML (either on the fly or in a batch mode). Thus HTML is a "representation" of the root XML document. Just as a music CD or tape is a representation of a master recording made with much more high-fidelity equipment, the display-oriented markup (HTML, WML, or whatever) is a representation for use by a consumer. As a consumer, you probably don't have an 18-track digital recording deck in your living room (or pocket). The CD or tape (or MP3 audio file, for that matter) is a representation of the original recording for you to take with you. But the music publisher retains the original master recording so that when a new medium comes out (like Super Audio CD, for instance), the publisher can convert the high-quality master to this new format. In the case of XML, you retain your XML data forever in your database, but what you send to consumers is markup specific to their current needs.

The Basics of XML

If you know HTML already, then you're familiar with the idea of tagging content. Tags are interspersed with data to represent "metadata" or data about the data. Let's start with the following sentence:

> Homer's Odyssey is a revered relic of the ancient world.

Imagine you never heard of the *Odyssey* or Homer. I'll reprint the sentence like this:

> Homer's <u>Odyssey</u> is a revered relic of the ancient world.

I've added metadata that adds meaning to the sentence. Just by adding one underline, I've loaded the sentence with extra meaning. In HTML, this sentence would be marked up like this:

```
Homer's <u>Odyssey</u> is a revered relic of the ancient world.
```

This markup indicates that the word "Odyssey" is to appear underlined. As described in the last section, HTML is really good only at describing layout—a display-oriented markup. If you're interested only in how users are *viewing* your sentences, that's great. However, if you want to give your documents part of a system, so that they can be managed intelligently and the content within them can be searched, sorted, filed, and repurposed to meet your business needs, you need to know more about them. A human can read the sentence and logically infer that the word "Odyssey" is a book title because of the underline. The sentence contains metadata (that is, the underline), but it's ambiguous to a computer and decodable only by the human reader. Why? Because computers are *stupid!* If you want a computer to know that "Odyssey" is a book title, you have to be much more explicit; this is where XML comes in. XML markup for the preceding sentence might be the following:

```
Homer's <book>Odyssey</book> is a revered relic of the ancient world.
```

Aha! Now we're getting somewhere. The document is marked up using a new tag, `<book>`, which I've made up just for this application, to indicate where book titles are referenced. This provides two important and powerful tools: You can centrally control the style of your documents, and you have machine-readable metadata—that is, a computer can easily examine your document and tell you where the references to book titles are. You can then choose to style the occurrences of book titles however you want—with underlines, in italics, in bold, with quotes around them, in a different color, whatever.

Let's say you want every book title you mention to be a hyperlink to a page that enables you to buy the book. The HTML markup would look something like this:

```
Homer's <u><a href="http://some.store.com/buybook.cgi?ISBN=0987-2343">Odyssey</a></u> is a revered relic of the ancient world.
```

In this example, you've *hard-coded* the document with a specific Uniform Resource Locator (URL) to a script on some online bookstore somewhere. What if that bookstore goes out of business? What if you make a strategic partnership with some other online bookstore and you want to change all the book titles to point to that store's pages? Then you've got to go through all of your documents with some kind of half-baked Perl script. What if your documents aren't all coded consistently? There are about a hundred things that can and will go wrong in this scenario. Believe me—I've been there.

Let's look at XML markup of the same sentence:

```
Homer's <book isbn="0987-2343">Odyssey</book> is a revered relic of the ancient world.
```

Now isn't that a breath of fresh air? By replacing the hard-coded script reference with a simple indication of ISBN (International Standard Book Number, a guaranteed unique number for every book printed[1]), you've cut the complexity of markup in half. In addition, you have enabled centralized control over whether book titles should be links and, if so, where they link. Assuming central control of how XML documents are turned into display-oriented markup, you can make a change in this one place to effect the display of many documents. As a special bonus, if you store all your XML documents in a database and properly *decompose*, or extract, the information within them (as we'll discuss next), you can also find out which book titles are referred to from which documents.

Why You Don't Need to Throw Away Your RDBMS

People often come up to me on the street and say, "Tell me, Dan, if I decide to build XML-based systems, what happens to my relational database?" A common misconception is that XML, as a new way of thinking about and representing data, means an end to the relational database management system (RDBMS) as we know it. Well, don't throw away your relational database just yet. XML is a way to format and bring order to data. By mating the power of XML with the immense and already well-understood power of SQL-based relational database systems, you get the best of both worlds. In the following chapters, I'll discuss some approaches to building this bridge between XML and your good old relational database.

Relational databases are great at some things (such as maintaining data integrity and storing highly structured data), while XML is great at other things (for example, formatting data for transmission, representing unstructured data, and ordering data). Using both XML and SQL (Structured Query Language) together enables you to use the best parts of both systems to create robust, data-centric systems. Together, XML and relational databases help you answer the fundamental question of content management and of data-oriented systems in general. That question is *"What do I have?"* Once you know what you have, you can do anything. If you don't know what you have, you

---

[1.] I realize that Homer's *Odyssey* has been reprinted thousands of times in many languages by different publishers and that all of the modern reprintings have their own ISBNs. This is simply an example.

essentially don't have anything. You'll see this question restated throughout this book in different ways.

A Brief Example

For convenience, let's say that I want to keep track of books by ISBN. ISBNs are convenient because they provide a unique numbering scheme for books. Let's take the previous example of the book references marked up by ISBN:

```
<document id="1">Homer's <book isbn="0987-2343">Odyssey</book> is a revered
relic of the ancient world.</document>
```

I've added `<document id="1">` and `</document>` tags around the body of my document so each document can uniquely identify itself. Each XML document I write has an ID number, which I've designated should be in a tag named "document" that wraps around the entire document. Again, remember that I'm just making these tags up. They're not a documented standard; they're just being used for the purpose of these examples.

For easy reference, I want to keep track of which ISBN numbers, are referred to from which documents; thus I design an SQL table to look something like this:

doc_id	ISBN
1	0987-2343
2	0872-8237

`doc_id` has referential integrity to a list of valid document ID numbers, and the `isbn` field has referential integrity to a list of valid ISBN numbers. "Great," I hear you saying, "this is a lot of complexity for a bunch of stupid book names. Explain to me *why* this is better than using HTML again."

Suppose I have a thousand documents (book reviews, articles, bulletin board messages, and so on), and I want to determine which of them refer to a specific book. In the HTML universe, I can perform a textual search for occurrences of the book name. But what if I have documents that refer to Homer's *Odyssey* and Arthur C. Clark's *2001: A Space Odyssey*? If I search for the word "odyssey," my search results list both books. However, if I've marked up all my references to books by ISBN and I've decomposed or extracted this information into a table in a database, I can use a *simple SQL query* to get the information I need quickly and reliably:

```
select doc_id from doc_isbn where isbn = '0987-2343'
```

The search results are a set of document ID numbers. I can choose to display the title of each document as a hyperlink, clickable to the actual document, or I can concatenate the documents and display them to the user one after another on a page—whatever the requirements of my application. By combining the power of XML machine-readable metadata with the simplicity and power of my relational database, I've created a powerful document retrieval tool that can answer the question, "What do I have?" Creating such a tool simply required a little forethought and designing skill.

If I'm going too fast for you, don't worry. I discuss these topics in detail in the following chapters.

Great! How Do I Get Started?

The four essential steps to building an XML-based system or application are the following:

1. Requirements gathering (described in Chapter 3)
2. Abstract data modeling (Chapter 4)
3. Application design, including DTD (document type definition) and schema design (Chapters 5 and 6)
4. Implementation (Chapters 8 and 9)

If you follow this plan, you won't write one line of application code until step 4. Building an XML-based application is writing software and requires the same rigorous approach.

The four steps don't mention platform at all. Are we implementing on UNIX or Windows NT? Oracle or MySql? Java or Perl? XML and database design free you from platform-dependent approaches to data storage and manipulation, so take advantage of that freedom, and don't even choose a platform until at least midway through step 2. Base that platform decision on what features it includes to get you closer to your goal—built-in features that fit into your business requirements—how easy the platform is to support ongoing operations (operational considerations).

You can incorporate the same methodology when integrating XML into an existing RDBMS-based application. Throughout the following chapters, we'll examine how to build an XML-based application. You'll learn how to collect your requirements, build an abstract data model around these requirements, and then build an XML DTD and a relational schema around this data model. We'll get into implementation only in the abstract, describing how your system must interact with the DTD and schema.

Summary

If I've done my job, you're excited about the raw potential of XML now. You've seen how it can work to turn dumb documents into smart documents—documents with oomph. You should understand where some of my passion for these systems comes from. I've seen them work and work well. In the next chapter, we'll step back into the history of both XML and the relational database to provide a bit more context before moving forward with application design and development.

Chapter 2

Introducing XML and SQL: A History Lesson of Sorts

> In which the compelling stories of the
> birth of our two heroes are revealed.

Before we delve into application design with XML and SQL, let's step back for a second to consider the historical context of these technologies. No technology is developed in a vacuum, and understanding their historical contexts can provide valuable insight into current and future architectural decisions that you have to make. If you're a judge who's trying to interpret some point of constitutional law, you need to understand the Founding Fathers' intentions. If you're writing literary criticism, you need to understand the author's time and circumstances to understand his or her work better. Likewise, to solve specific problems of their times, people build technology standards. It pays to understand the context before you start fooling around with these technologies.

Extensible Markup Language (XML)

From reading the last chapter, you already know that XML is the best thing since sliced bread, but to set the scene more accurately, let's go back to the origins of XML and find out what it's really all about.

The design goals for XML (lifted from the text of the XML specification current at this writing—XML 1.0 Second Edition[1]are as follows:

1. XML shall be straightforwardly usable over the Internet.
2. XML shall support a wide variety of applications.
3. XML shall be compatible with SGML.
4. It shall be easy to write programs that process XML documents.
5. The number of optional features in XML is to be kept to the absolute minimum, ideally zero.
6. XML documents should be human legible and reasonably clear.
7. The XML design should be prepared quickly.
8. The design of XML shall be formal and concise.
9. XML documents shall be easy to create.
10. Terseness in XML markup is of minimal importance.

The XML specification was written by the the World Wide Web Consortium (W3C), the body that develops and recommends Web specifications and standards. Tim Berners-Lee founded the W3C in 1994 because he thought there might be something to the little information retrieval system he built while working as a research physicist at Switzerland's CERN laboratory. The W3C's membership has since climbed to over 500 member organizations. In 1994 the Hypertext Markup Language (HTML) was in its infancy, having been built hastily on top of the Standard Generalized Markup Language (SGML). SGML, in turn, had become an international standard in 1986 when it was made so by the International Standards Organization (ISO). Actually it was based on the Generalized Markup Language (GML), developed in 1969 at IBM.

In 1996, the members of the W3C undertook what would become their most influential project: the creation of a new language for the Web, called eXtensi-

---

[1.] XML 1.0 Second Edition is available at http://www.w3.org/TR/2000/REC-xml-20001006.

ble Markup Language (or XML for short). XML was related to SGML, but instead of defining a specific tag set as HTML does, XML enables the designer of a system to create tag sets to support specific domains of knowledge—academic disciplines such as physics, mathematics, and chemistry, and business domains such as finance, commerce, and journalism. XML is a subset of SGML. Like SGML, it is a set of rules for building markup languages. Each of XML's rules is also a rule of SGML.

XML and languages like it use tags to indicate structure within a piece of text. Here's a simple bit of XML-compliant HTML as an example:

```
<p>Homer's <u>Odyssey</u> is a really nice book.</p>
```

The portion of the text between the matching <u> begin tag and the </u> end tag is marked up, or slated, for whatever treatment we deem appropriate for the <u> tag (in the case of HTML, an underline). The result is

>   Homer's <u>Odyssey</u> is a really nice book.

This tag structure is hierarchical; that is, you can place tags inside of tags as shown in Figure 2-1.

Figure 2-1 renders like this:

>   Homer's <u>Odyssey</u> is *a **really nice** book.*[2]

The horizontal rules in Figure 2-1 indicate the basic tag structure. The <p> tag encloses the whole sentence. Inside the two <p> tags are two other tags, <u> and <em>, and inside of <em> is a <strong> tag, three levels down. Tags can go inside of tags, but tags must match up at the same "level." Hence, the following is not well-formed XML:

```
<p>Homer's <u>Odyssey</u> is <em>a <strong>really nice</em></strong> book.</p>
```

[2.] In this example, I'm assuming you have some knowledge of HTML tags. Just in case you're not familiar with them, or you need a quick refresher, the <p> tag (paragraph tag) encloses the entire sentence. Inside the two <p> tags are two other tags, <u> (underline) and <em> (emphasis) tags.

```
<p>Homer's <u>Odyssey</u> is <em>a <strong>really nice</strong> book.</em></p>
```

Figure 2-1: XML's hierarchical tag structure

The previous example has an <em> tag and within it a <strong> tag, but the <em> tag is ended before the <strong> tag it contains. It isn't well formed because an XML document is not a document at all, but a tree. Let's take the well-formed example in Figure 2-1 and visualize it as a tree (see Figure 2-2).

As you can see in Figure 2-2, each part of the example sentence is represented in a leaf or *node* of this tree. The tree structure is a basic data type that a computer can easily deal with. A computer program can "traverse" a tree by starting at the top and making its way down the left branch first. Then, when it gets to a dead end, it goes up a level and looks for a right branch, and so on, until it gets to the very last, rightmost leaf. This kind of traversal is the most elementary kind of computer science, which is why XML is such a wonderful way to represent data in the machine world.

Evaluating XML's Design Goals

How did XML's authors do on their list of initial design goals? Let's take a look.

1. **XML shall be straightforwardly usable over the Internet.** The meaning of this goal is a bit fuzzy, but the W3C was essentially going for coherence between XML and other already-existing forms of information retrieval that occur on the Internet, specifically, HTML. The goal may also mean that XML wouldn't be proprietary or proprietary software would not be required to use it. In other words, XML documents should be usable by a broad audience; they should be completely open, not proprietary and closed. No real worries there. Another important factor in being straightforwardly usable over the Internet is that documents should be self-contained. In particular, XML documents can be processed without the presence of a DTD (see

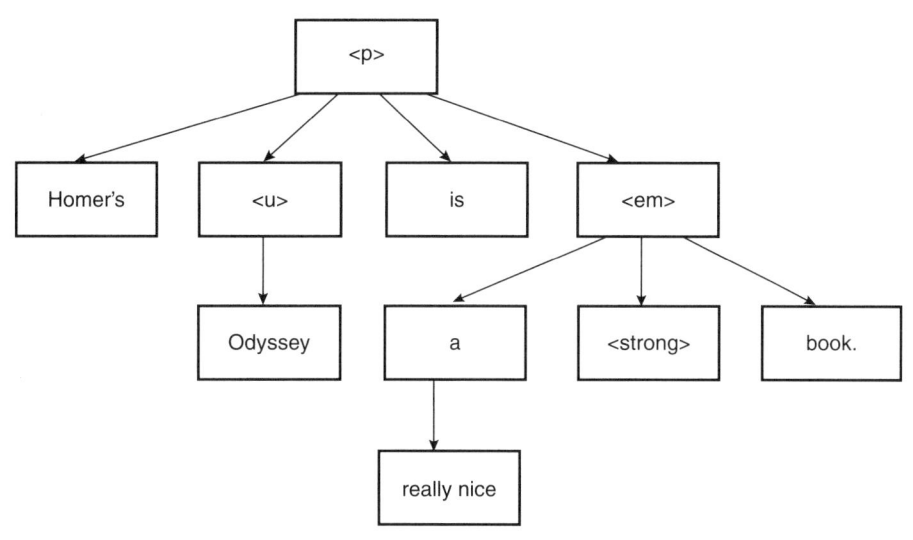

Figure 2-2: The hierarchical layout of our XML example

Chapter 5), in contrast to SGML where a DTD is always necessary to make sense of documents. Self-contained documents are important in an environment based on request/response protocols (such as HTTP, the information protocol underlying the World Wide Web) where communications failures are common.

2. **XML shall support a wide variety of applications.** As already discussed, XML can support any number of applications, ranging from different human disciplines (chemistry, news, math, finance, law, and so on) to machine-to-machine transactions, such as online payment and content syndication. Put a big check mark in the box on this one.

3. **XML shall be compatible with SGML.** XML is based on the SGML specification (as described in the XML 1.0 W3C Recommendation document as a "dialect of SGML"), so the W3C has also met this design goal.

4. **It shall be easy to write programs that process XML documents.** Because XML is a simplified form of SGML, it's even easier to write programs that process XML documents than it is to write programs that process SGML.

5. **The number of optional features in XML is to be kept to the absolute minimum, ideally zero.** By "optional" features, the W3C refers to some variations of SGML that include so-called optional features used only in certain SGML applications. These variations complicate SGML parsers and processors and ultimately mean that some SGML parsers aren't compatible with some SGML documents. In other words, all SGML is compatible, but some SGML applications are *more* compatible than others. The original XML working group members recognized that XML couldn't suffer from this kind of fragmentation, or it would go the way of SGML and become an obscure and abstruse language used only by information professionals.

   XML actually does have some optional features, which means, in theory, that you can get different results depending on what parser you use to read a document. However, in my experience you won't have to worry about XML's optional features, and they're certainly not within the scope of this book, so we won't go into them here.

6. **XML documents should be human legible and reasonably clear.** The best the W3C has been able to do is to make it easy for XML documents to be human legible. Because XML by its very nature enables anyone to design and implement an XML-based vocabulary, the W3C can't guarantee that all XML documents will be human readable. At least you have a fighting chance, however, because XML is a text-based format rather than a binary format like GIF of PDF.

   Later efforts by the W3C have diverged from this goal. Flip forward to Chapter 6, where I discuss XML Schema, and you'll see what I mean—it doesn't mean that XML Schema is a bad thing; it's just not immediately human readable. As with a programming language, you have to understand what you're looking at. So it's 50/50 on readability, but maybe this goal wasn't realistic in the first place.

7. **The XML design should be prepared quickly.** Compared with other international standards efforts, such as ISO standards that often take years and sometimes decades to complete and publish, the W3C certainly did a bang-up job on this goal. It took a year to produce the first draft. Put a check mark next to this goal.

8. **The design of XML shall be formal and concise.** The XML specification is definitely formal; it is derived from SGML in a formal,

declarative sense. The *Cambridge International Dictionary of English* defines *concise* as "expressing what needs to be said without unnecessary words." According to this definition, I'd say the specification is concise in that it includes everything that needs to be there without any extraneous material. Of course, conciseness is in the eye of the beholder. If you read through the specification, "concise" may not be the first word that comes to mind.

9. **XML documents shall be easy to create.** You can author an XML document in any text editor, so put a check mark next to this goal.

10. **Terseness in XML markup is of minimal importance.** This tenth requirement speaks volumes and represents the fundamental shift that the information science and computer industry have gone through during the 1980s and 1990s. At the dawn of the computer age, terseness was of primary importance. Those familiar with the Y2K uproar will understand the consequences of this propensity for terseness. In the name of terseness, software engineers used abbreviated dates (01/01/50 rather than 01/01/1950) in many of the systems they wrote. This presented later problems when the year 2000 rolled around because computer systems couldn't be certain if a date was 1950 or 2050. Amazingly, this practice lasted until the late 1990s, when some embedded systems that had the so-called "two-digit date" problem were still being produced.

We can laugh now, but quite a lot of otherwise smart people found themselves holed up in bunkers clutching AK-47s and cans of baked beans and feeling a little silly about it all at five minutes past midnight on January 1, 2000.

To be fair, the reason systems were designed with the two-digit date wasn't because the software engineers were dumb; it was because memory and storage were expensive in the 1970s and 1980s. It's easy now to say that they should have known better, now that storage and bandwidth are comparatively cheap and easy to obtain and people routinely download and store hours of digitized music on their home computers.

This "tenth commandment" of XML is essentially saying "out with the old" thinking where protocols and data formats had to be designed based on available storage and bandwidth resources. Now that such storage and bandwidth are available and are becoming ubiquitous in our lives, the W3C wanted to avoid having storage and bandwidth be factors in the design of XML.

The implications of storage and bandwidth are easy to overlook, but they're quite important in the way information systems are designed and implemented, and they will have repercussions for years to come.

Bandwidth Strikes Back: Mobile Devices

One way in which bandwidth is rearing its ugly head once again is through the proliferation of mobile-connected devices (such as WAP phones and e-mail devices like Research In Motion's Blackberry two-way pager). The wireless connections these devices use are generally pretty low bandwidth; current Global System for Mobile Communications (GSM, the mobile/cellular phone standard in use in most of the world), mobile phones, and infrastructure are mostly limited to 9600 baud. E-mail devices like Blackberry use paging networks that aren't "always on" and allow only small packets of data to be received discontinuously.

Yet industry pundits like Steve Ballmer of Microsoft are predicting XML to be the lingua franca of all connected mobile devices. Indeed, WML, the language WAP phones speak, is based on XML, and the languages that are lined up to replace it are also based on XML.

This bandwidth issue will go away for mobile devices, eventually. We're already seeing more high-bandwidth networks and devices being deployed, especially in high-tech strongholds. People who are currently trying to solve this bandwidth issue treat it as if it's the major limiting factor for mobile device proliferation. These efforts are misguided. The real killer apps for mobile devices will be multimedia broadband applications, and these applications will drive an explosion in bandwidth, just as they have for wired networks.

Structured Query Language (SQL)

The history of Structured Query Language (SQL) and the history of XML actually have a lot in common. SQL is a language for accessing data in a relational database. Relational databases are accessed (that is, they are queried) using SQL commands.

What Is "Relational"?

Relational databases store data in table structures; this is a very simple idea. A table has rows and columns. In a relational database table, each row is a single "item" (or *instance*) of the subject represented by the table, and each column is a value or *attribute* of a specific data type (for example, integer, string, Boolean) associated with that item. A "relation" is a table composed of these rows and columns. An example of a relational table follows:

Book_ID (*Integer*)	Book_Title (*String*)
1	Moby Dick
2	Sense and Sensibility
3	Pride and Prejudice

This book table, a relational table of book titles, has two columns (one for a book ID number and one for a book title).

The word "relational" is often confused with another aspect of relational databases: the ability to construct *relations* between different tables through the use of references. Say we have a table of authors, such as the one that follows:

Author_ID (*Integer*)	Author_Name (*String*)
1	Herman Melville
2	Jane Austen

If I want to include authors in the book table, I can include them by adding a reference between the book table and the author table, as follows:

Book_ID (*Integer*)	Book_Title (*String*)	Book_Author (*Integer*)
1	Moby Dick	1
2	Sense and Sensibility	2
3	Pride and Prejudice	2

Because the `Book_Author` column of the new book table is an integer value, relating back to the author table, the database now "knows" which books were written by the same author. I can ask the database to "list all books written by Jane Austen," and it can give me a sensible answer:

```
select Book.Book_ID, Book.Book_Title, Author.Author_Name
  from Book, Author
  where Book.Book_Author = Author.AuthorID
  and Author.Author_Name = 'Jane Austen'
```

The preceding question (or query) is written in SQL. It's called a *join* because it's a query that joins together two tables. The answer comes back from the database as—ta da—another table:

Book_ID	Book_Title	Author_Name
2	Sense and Sensibility	Jane Austen
3	Pride and Prejudice	Jane Austen

Referential Integrity

One of the most-loved aspects of relational databases is their ability to keep *referential integrity* between tables. Referential integrity means that, if your database is designed correctly, it becomes impossible to insert invalid data into it. Taking the previous example, I couldn't insert a row into the book table with an `Author_ID` of 3 because no author with an ID of 3 is listed in the author table. First I'm required to insert the new author into the author table; only then can I refer to it from the book table. The ability to maintain referential integrity is one of the most useful and powerful features of SQL databases. In Chapter 6 we'll delve further into this topic and, specifically, how it can help you build XML applications.

Note

I've simplified the previous example to make my point about references. If you were building this application the right way, you would construct a total of three tables: the book table, the author table, and then a "bridging table" between the two (called something like "author_book" or "book_author"), which would contain references to both tables. Why? What if you had a book that was coauthored by two authors who otherwise had authored books on their own or with other authors? Which author would the entry in your book table contain? If you build your table as I've done in the previous example, you'll limit yourself to books with only one author, or you'll be able to look up only the "primary" author of a book. Best to create a separate table that contains references to both your book and author tables—a bridging table. This concept will be expanded further when we get to data modeling in Chapter 4.

Relational databases are big into tables and for good reason. Tables are another kind of data structure that is easy for computers to deal with. Even the simplest computer languages contain the concept of an *array*, a numbered sequence of values. A table is simply a multidimensional array—two dimensions to be precise—an array of arrays.

SQL was originally created by IBM, after which many vendors developed versions of SQL. Early in the 1980s, the American National Standards Institute (ANSI) started developing a relational database language standard. ANSI and the International Standards Organization (ISO) published SQL standards in 1986 and 1987, respectively. In 1992, ISO and ANSI ratified the SQL-92 standard, which is used for SQL examples throughout this book.

Fitting It All Together

Let's take a look at a rough timeline of events starting in 1969 when GML came into use at IBM (see Figure 2-3).

Surprisingly, the historical roots of XML go back further than those of SQL. Not that much further, though, and remember that nonrelational databases were around long before 1969.

XML data maps best onto trees. SQL data maps best onto arrays. These approaches are two totally different ways of looking at the world.

Those of you familiar with high school physics will know that as light travels through space it can be thought of as both a wave and a stream of particles (photons). Both of these views make sense, both are internally consistent, and predictions based on both views yield reproducible results. The question of whether light "really is" a particle or "really is" a wave is irrelevant and meaningless. Both the wave and the particle view are simply frameworks that we

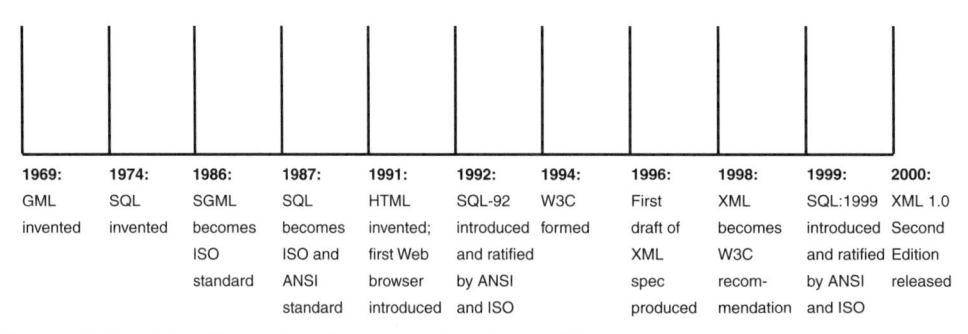

1969:	1974:	1986:	1987:	1991:	1992:	1994:	1996:	1998:	1999:	2000:
GML invented	SQL invented	SGML becomes ISO standard	SQL becomes ISO and ANSI standard	HTML invented; first Web browser introduced	SQL-92 introduced and ratified by ANSI and ISO	W3C formed	First draft of XML spec produced	XML becomes W3C recommendation	SQL:1999 introduced and ratified by ANSI and ISO	XML 1.0 Second Edition released

Figure 2-3: Timeline of major events in SQL and XML

apply to make sense of reality, and both can be useful in predicting and understanding the universe.

Likewise, both relational databases and more object-oriented views of data such as XML can be applied to make sense of and process the vast amounts of information around us. Both approaches are useful in the process of delivering information to a user.

And that's what it's all about, isn't it? You can build a sublimely engineered information processing and retrieval system, but at the end of the day, it's the user's needs that have to drive the design of an application. The user always comes first, which is why, as we'll see in Chapter 3, gathering requirements is so important.

A Note on Standards

> *The great thing about standards is that there are so many of them.*
>
> —A maxim sometimes attributed to Andrew Tannenbaum, professor of computer science at Vrije Universiteit in the Netherlands.

Understanding the world of international standards and standards bodies, especially in the IT family of industries, is a daunting task. In this journey of discovery, it pays to remember that the existence of international standards is responsible for the emergence of the industrial and information ages. Your Scandinavian mobile phone works in Hong Kong. You can ship a package from Barcelona to Fiji. You can access Web pages for AOL, Microsoft, Sun, and Sony. Systems built on top of international standards power this planet.

Going back to our first example of XML in Chapter 1, we used an ISBN (International Standardized Book Number) to identify Homer's *Odyssey* uniquely. The ISBN is based on a standard from the ISO (the International Organization for Standardization). ISO is the granddaddy of standards organizations, but many other standards bodies and organizations exist to develop, publish, and/or promote international standards. SQL is an ISO standard, but most Web standards aren't from ISO because of the length of time it takes to develop an ISO standard.

The W3C (World Wide Web Consortium—http://www.w3.org) is the home of most Web standards. Many people don't understand the relevancy of this powerful body. The W3C is a "member organization"; that is, the people who participate in the W3C standards efforts are representatives of member organizations and corporations, the same bodies that implement and use these standards.

Two kinds of standards exist in the real world. *De jure*[3] standards ("from law") are documents created and approved by formal standards bodies (for example, SGML, XML, and HTML). *De facto* standards ("from fact") are no more than standards that come into being through common usage: They are standards because so many people use them (for example, the GIF image format, the ZIP compression format, WAP, and Word's "DOC" file format). Some de facto standards (such as WAP) have strong lobby organizations that promote their use, but that doesn't make them any less "de facto."

Both types of standards are important, and it's essential to note that something can be a "standard" without having been ratified by the ISO. And de facto standards are often supported better. For instance, Macromedia's proprietary Flash product is pervasive on the Web, but Scalable Vector Graphics (SVG), which is supported by the W3C, is currently implemented only on the W3C's own test bed Amaya browser.

Summary

Now you have some of the history for both XML and SQL and some insight into the high-flying world of international standards. It's valuable to understand how these languages were conceived and for what purposes they were developed, but that's not to say that they can't be put to other uses. Standards, de facto or otherwise, breed other, more complex and exciting standards and uses. For example, without standards (TCP/IP, Ethernet, SMTP e-mail, POP, HTTP, and so on), the Internet as we know it never would have developed. The participants in each of those individual standards efforts were focused on solving one particular problem, not on building a global network. Standards create new markets and spur progress.

Now let's learn how to put the standards of XML and SQL to work.

[3.] Not to be confused with "du jour" standard (standard of the day). It often feels as if you're dealing with a "du jour" standard when you're using Web standards of any kind. For instance, in putting together this book, I've had to contend with the rapidly evolving XML and SQL standards.

Chapter 3

Project Definition and Management

> In which the King of Sweden learns a valuable lesson about project scoping.

In this chapter, we explore the topics of project definition and project management, particularly as they relate to small- to medium-sized projects. I'm taking a pragmatic approach to these topics, based on my own experiences within the New Media sector. We'll start with project definition, that is, understanding the problem you're trying to solve. This discussion revolves largely around capturing *requirements*. We then move on to topics that are significant in the execution of your project: project management and quality assurance.

An Illustrative Anecdote

In 1623, in the midst of a war with the Catholic Poles, the King of Sweden, King Gustav Adolphus II, launched his most formidable and impressive battleship, the *Vasa*. The ship was festooned with carvings and ornate structures that were intended to intimidate his enemy into retreat. Unfortunately, 15 minutes into its maiden voyage, amid much fanfare and pageantry, the *Vasa* keeled over and sank to the bottom of Stockholm's harbor, killing about 30 of its crewmen and astounding a shocked throng that was keen to celebrate the king's newly christened flagship.

The designer (who had died during the *Vasa's* construction) was blamed for having designed the ship with too little ballast, but recently, a new theory is gaining ground as to the real reason for the *Vasa's* demise. After the designer died, King Adolphus decided that he wanted a second row of gun ports (where the cannons stick out) added to the ship. Apparently, he had seen an English ship with this configuration and simply *had* to have it on his new flagship. The ship was designed to accommodate only one row of gun ports; of course, no one wanted to tell that to the king. More gun ports equals more guns equals a top-heavy ship.

The ship was raised and refloated in 1961 and now sits in a museum in Stockholm where tourists can marvel at this 300-year-old monument to *scope creep*.

Scope creep is the tendency for projects to start small, seemingly well defined, and then become big, complex, and poorly documented by the end. Scope creep is the single most intractable problem software developers must deal with because its roots are tied up in issues of interpersonal communications, expectation management, and psychology, among other issues. In short, understanding and managing scope creep are human disciplines, not a matter of ones and zeros, and it requires a different set of skills than those that must be applied to designing software and writing code. Scope creep is sometimes exacerbated because people with otherwise good intentions start projects without documenting requirements in sufficient detail. Good requirements gathering and documentation of those requirements are essential in order to manage scope creep. I say "manage" and not "eliminate" because scope creep is inherent in any project.

In the e-business world, requirements often shift underneath you while you're working. Just as King Adolphus decided late into the project that he needed one more row of gun ports, your internal or external customer may decide that his requirements have to change. How do you avoid your project ending up at the bottom of the harbor 15 minutes after launch? Proper project management keeps a project on track. Be true to the requirements originally set out, but be nimble enough to react and change—to roll with the punches.

How to Capture Requirements

A requirement, in systems and software development terms, is just that, a required piece of functionality. Implicit in the word *requirement*, however, is a relationship among people. Understanding that relationship and your role in it is key to the process of effectively gathering requirements. The process of requirements gathering requires customer orientation, even if that "customer" is an internal one. The customer is always right, as the phrase goes. That doesn't mean you do everything the customer says. You have to lead your customer through the process of definition of requirements, all the while nimbly jumping in and out of his mind set.

It's important to keep in mind that computer systems and applications are built for *people*. These people (generally referred to as *users*) have needs and aspirations. They have *expectations*—expectations that, if not met, result in the users' disappointment. The phrase "managing expectations" has become de rigueur among engineering departments, but the first step in managing customer expectations is to document the basic requirements and present them to the customer. This is the beginning of a conversation between you and the customer. In order to start this conversation, you need to understand who your users are, what motivates them, what frustrates them, what makes them tick.

We discuss strategies for getting to know your users when I introduce the CyberCinema example later in the chapter. Some of this stuff might seem pretty basic, but it's amazing how many projects get fouled up beyond all recognition (to borrow a phrase from World War II) because of a lack of basic understanding of requirements.

If you're already an expert on how to gather requirements and build requirements documents, you can probably skip this chapter. However, you may want to read the section CyberCinema: The Adventure Begins so you'll be familiar with an example that I use in subsequent chapters.

So what are requirements? Let's start with a brief example: a simple e-mail system. For this application, we want a group of users to be able to write e-mail messages to each other. These messages should have a short summary (a subject line) and a message body.

"Simple! Hand me that compiler, and we'll get started," you say.

Bad developer! No biscuit! First you must distill the requirements into a simple set of sentences, each encompassing a single requirement. They might look something like this:

- A user must be able to write an e-mail message.
- A user must be able to send e-mail to another user.
- A user must be able to read e-mail sent from another user.
- An e-mail consists of a subject line and a message body.

Notice how abstract these requirements are. We're not talking about what the user sees, where the message appears, what gets clicked on, what noises the user hears when he or she receives mail, or anything like that. These are important parts of application design, but the foundations (that is, what you start with) are the basic, abstract requirements.

Keeping these requirements abstract and divorced from considerations of user interface will help you throughout your application development cycle. For example, you may decide to change application environments halfway through your project. Testing may reveal that some initial assumption about expected performance doesn't hold true or that your planned user interface framework isn't as easy to use as you thought it would be. Application requirements developed in the abstract mean that you can apply them to whatever environment you wish.

In an ideal situation, you gather these requirements before making any vendor or product choices, which affords you maximum flexibility in making these choices. You may find, through the requirements capture process, that some of your assumptions about what you need aren't valid. For instance, I worked with a client who was obsessed with the question, "What content management system should I buy?" Working with the client, I turned the question around: What did the client hope to accomplish? Before making a commitment on a software product that could cost upwards of $100,000, the company needed to take a look at their requirements. It's possible they may not have needed a packaged content management solution at all. Working out abstract requirements up front keeps you nimble, saves you money, and focuses your attention on the important issues in building your application: your users' expectations.

Working with this basic set of requirements, you can then build a more robust requirements document that talks about user interface, deployment, and so on. For instance, the user can click on a button labeled "send new e-mail message" with a smiley face on it, which brings up a window that . . . You get the idea.

CyberCinema: The Adventure Begins

Throughout this book, we will use a fictitious Web site, CyberCinema, as an example. Let's say an ambitious entrepreneur has managed to bamboozle some venture capitalists out of a few million bucks to help him start his business: an online movie review site. Maybe he just quit his job as a movie reviewer at a prestigious national newspaper. He knows all about movie reviews and the film industry. He's hired a talented editorial staff, a designer, and one techie—that's you.

Your mission is to create the technical infrastructure for this company. The immediate requirements are clear: Build the Web site. But you know from talking to your new boss that you may want to syndicate these movie reviews to other Web sites as well. You may want to push them out to WAP phones or other wireless devices, or you may want people to be able to dial a phone number and listen to a review being read aloud. Of course, because you're a discerning engineer, the thing that immediately springs to mind is all the beer you'll be able to afford once your options vest. The second thing that springs to mind is that this looks like a job for XML.

How right you are!

One of your technical challenges is to build a publishing system for the movie reviews. First, you must assemble a set of requirements. Because you're not an expert in movie reviews, where should you go to find these requirements? You could buy every book ever written by Leonard Maltin, but you'll probably be better off consulting your user community, the review writers. By synthesizing the requirements of the writers (who will use the system from the inside) and the design of the Web site (which is the outward-facing view to the world), you can assemble a reliable set of basic requirements.

Requirements Gathering

My method of gathering requirements is simple: Lock everyone together in a room, lead the discussion, encourage the participants to talk to each other, and listen. Make sure everyone with any sway over decision making is in this room. If your new boss decides at the last minute to skip the meeting to talk to some investment bankers in Chicago, cancel the meeting and reschedule it. It can be difficult getting all the key people together in one room, but it's essential. If necessary, use bribery. Offer pizza, serve drinks, and bake cookies; give the participants gifts. Any personal expense incurred is a good investment in your future employability. You want to write a list of raw requirements that everyone agrees to. I recommend using a large easel with paper sheets that can be torn away so you can write down key points where everyone can see them.

Suppose during the discussion one of the writers says, "Users should be able to search movies by title." You should write "movies searchable by title" on your big sheet of paper to get the designer thinking and subsequently offering another idea. As things get proposed, shot down, and so forth, you're contributing, but you're also keeping a running tally of what was said. Periodically you should go through the points raised so far and invite further discussion on each point.

User Scenarios

A problem with these types of sessions is that the participants often bring with them their own preconceived notions of what "the system" should do. It's incredibly difficult to get the participants to step back from these ideas and think about the actual requirements in a more abstract form. One tactic I've used with some success is to structure the conversation in the form of scenarios or "user stories." These aren't the same as "use cases," which we'll get to later (see the sidebar, Formal Use Case Analysis with Unified Modeling Language (UML), later in this chapter). They're broad-brush narrative form, "day-in-the-life" stories about how people actually conduct their lives.

If these stories are used correctly, the rest of the requirements flow easily from them.

First, it's important to understand who your users are. In the case of this "movie review" content management, we're talking mostly about the people involved in the production of the reviews, but we also have to talk about the users of the site—the end users—who eventually will read these reviews. If we don't include them in our user scenarios, it's going to be difficult to figure out what information needs to be captured by our content management system. In the real world, companies have vast storehouses of demographic data on their customers, but they often don't put this data to work for them during the software development process. Because we are talking about two groups of users (internal and external), I recommend doing two sessions: one to determine the end-user requirements and the second to delve further into the content management and workflow requirements of the review writers. You should do your end-user–oriented (customer-oriented) scenarios *first*, before doing internal user scenarios. This might seem obvious, but it's amazing how many organizations make the simple mistake of considering their internal users before their customer-oriented users. If you don't fully understand how your customers are going to interact with your system, there's no way you're going to know how to construct internal systems to meet their needs.

If you don't have enough information on your potential users, don't be afraid to run focus groups. It may seem namby-pamby because running focus groups is sometimes seen as passing the buck, but you can save yourself considerable time and frustration by starting with a clear idea of who your users are. What are their daily lives like? What is their technical skill level? Are they early adopters? Do they have fast computers? Are your internal users a bunch of Internet morons who would be more at home with a quill pen than a mouse?

Our user story for the CyberCinema site might look something like this:

User Story

Joe enjoys going to movies at the cinema. He's 27 years old and has a fast Internet connection at home. In the subway one day he sees an ad for a new movie review site. At work, he visits this site during his lunch break. He's looking for a review of a David Lynch film that just came out, although he doesn't remember the title of the film. He brings up the home page, which features reviews of top box-office films. The page contains a list of latest releases, including listings of actors and directors. He notices that the actors' and directors' names are "clickable," but he decides to click on the film title instead. He's presented with a summary of this film, along with an expected release date and a note that a more detailed review will be available later in the day. He is invited to register to receive an update on his mobile phone when the review becomes available. Joe registers with the site and enters his mobile phone information, after which he is returned to the same page. Joe now notices that the name "David Lynch" is clickable. He clicks it, and a filmography of David Lynch, along with a short biography of the director, is displayed. Joe doesn't recognize one of the films on the list, so he clicks on its title. He is presented with a review, which he reads. Since this film is on video, Joe follows a link that enables him to buy it from an online movie retailer.

On his way home from work, Joe gets a message on his mobile phone, alerting him that a review and a summary for the David Lynch film are now on the site. At home he brings up a Web browser and types the URL given to him on his mobile phone to access the review. He reads the review and then follows a link to book tickets at a theater for the following night. Going back to the review, he notices that the name of one of the actresses is clickable. He clicks on the name to see a full biography and filmography of this actress. He then clicks on the title of one of the other films, which, based on the review, he decides to buy on DVD.

Notice that the user story doesn't mention how the Web page looks, what colors are on the screen, and so on. The story is about what Joe uses the application for and how it affects his life. Now let's look at our second user story, the story of the movie reviewer, that is, the internal customer.

User Story

Susan writes film reviews for CyberCinema. She is a computer power user, comfortable with her PC, working in a team of five reviewers for a lead editor. She finds a message on her PC at work noting that the lead editor has assigned her to write reviews for five films. Based on earlier conversations with her lead editor, Susan has notes for four of these film reviews, which she writes up immediately. She writes each review separately and submits them all to the lead editor. She hasn't watched David Lynch's latest film, so she leaves that one for the last, knowing that she'll be able to see an early screening later in the day. As she's finishing her fourth review, her first and second reviews come back to her with edits and suggestions from the lead editor. She makes the suggested changes and sends the reviews back to the lead editor. In one review, she mentions a previous review that she wrote of a similar film. She also annotates each mention of an actor or actress appropriately.

Requirements Gathering Tips and Techniques

Understanding and recording users' requirements is much more an art than a science. Doing it correctly takes patience, an understanding of your customers' needs, a willingness to reach beyond differences in communicative styles between you and your customers, knowledge of systems architectures, and a willingness to step beyond your knowledge of systems architecture to look at the big picture.

Here are some basic dos and don'ts to keep in mind during the process:

- When capturing requirements (for instance, in the types of sessions described previously), *do* lead the conversation. Your time and your users' time are precious. Don't let fringe issues sidetrack the discussion.

- Never guess blindly at what the user wants. Always ask, or at least make an educated guess based on your user intelligence. If you forget to cover an issue during this session, you will be tempted to gloss over it and make assumptions based on the way you envision them working. Don't do this; you will almost always be wrong. Always go back to the users and ask them, even if it is a pain.

- Don't get bogged down in technical details. Stay away from phrases like "the system," especially during the first part of the discussion. Don't talk about what the users want "the system" to do. Instead talk about how they live their lives; user stories will flow naturally from those discussions.

- When you do start getting to the concrete (such as user interface design), try to be visual. Draw a rough "screen flow" to help users understand how they're going to interact with the application.

- Prioritize as you go. It's good practice to start by talking about a phased approach, which is especially important when you're planning to use one of the interactive development methods described later in this chapter (see the section Project Management). Organize features to be implemented in phase 1, phase 2, and so forth. This doesn't mean your list will necessarily be the rollout schedule, but it provides an idea of the priorities.

- Avoid *groupthink*. Groupthink is the tendency for a group of people to sit around a table and nod their heads when they're really thinking "that will never work, but everyone else is nodding his head, so I must be wrong." You can single out people to respond to your questions as a tactic for avoiding groupthink: "Bob, you seem unsure of that, do you have an opinion to the contrary?" Even if Bob doesn't have a contrary opinion, you've indicated that it's okay to have a contrary opinion.
- Finally, one last requirements tidbit: Users will sacrifice features for ease-of-use, but don't expect them not to complain about it later. If you want to be the "good guy," underpromise and overdeliver.

At the end of this session, you should have not only the user stories, but a bunch of big pieces of paper with a lot of other notes written on them. Save these notes, and hang them on the partition walls of your cubicle where you can continually refer to them. Six months down the road, when someone storms in and asks you, "Why doesn't our system do X?" you can point to a note and say, "Show me X on our list of requirements." Aside from merely providing a means of justifying your actions, keeping these notes enables you to refer back to this original "document" throughout the development process, without fear that something was lost in transcription.

Conversational Style

Differences in *conversational style* is an important issue to keep in mind during requirements gathering. Cultural differences, gender differences, whether you grew up with siblings are only some of the factors that can impact conversational style. If one of your users seems aggressive or combative during the requirements gathering phase, your first impulse might be to tune him or her out. If the user is so aggressive that he or she is not letting others have their say, it can be a problem. But try to remember that the ways people are raised and their cultures dictate their communicative styles. For example, while dealing with an Irish colleague during a day-long meeting, I thought he was interrupting me. He would talk and then stop talking. I then would start talking, either to respond to him or to clarify, but he immediately would start talking over me. It became very annoying, and over the course of the morning, I began to feel hostile toward him. I thought he was a jerk, and I disregarded what he had to say.

Midway through the day, I realized what was happening: He was pausing between sentences for longer periods than I was used to. This lengthy pause was possibly due to a cultural difference between a fast-talking New Yorker and a laid-back Irishman (although I've known some fast-talking Irishmen). He wasn't constantly interrupting me; *I* was interrupting *him*. I nearly fell out of my chair; in retrospect it was so obvious. Armed with my new insight, I made myself wait him out, and, wonder of wonders, it worked. He was able to finish his sentences. I listened to him, and he listened to me.

This kind of thing happens all the time, both in and out of the workplace. Part of the solution is to develop listening skills. Learn to check yourself when you're not listening, when you find yourself waiting for someone to stop talking instead of actually listening to what he or she is saying, for instance.

For more discussion on communicative styles, in the workplace and in personal relationships as well, I recommend *That's Not What I Meant: How Conversational Style Makes or Breaks Relationships* by Deborah Tannen (1991).

Functional Requirements Document

The next step is to build a functional requirements document from all this information and the user requirements. The functional requirements document encapsulates everything in the user stories and the meeting notes. In the case of our CyberCinema site, the core of this document must be the abstract requirements, which might look something like this:

1. Reviewers must be able to write reviews.
2. Reviews can contain normal text features such as bold, italic, and underline.
3. Reviews can include headings to delineate one section of a review from another.
4. In reviews, actor names, movie names, and director names must be links to a search facility of some kind.
5. Reviews can contain links to other reviews.
6. Reviews can contain links to outside URLs.
7. Reviews must be searchable by movie.
8. Reviews must be searchable by director.

9. Reviews must be searchable by actor.
10. Reviews must be searchable by reviewer.
11. Movies must be searchable by director.
12. Movies must be searchable by actor.

For simplicity's sake, I've left out some requirements, but you get the idea. One approach might be to present the requirements in the document within the context of the user story. I recommend building a two-column document, with excerpts from the user story in the left column and corresponding requirements statements in the right column, as shown in Figure 3-1.

You then might flesh out these requirements with annotated rough interface mockups like the one shown in Figure 3-2.

It's important not to get too specific about the user interface here. For example, in Figure 3-2, I put in a box for "Navigation Area," but I haven't specified what will be in that area. You're trying to get a rough idea of how the interface will work, not pin down every last detail. (That's where you get into site design and information architecture, which are out of the scope of this book.) If you're interested in these topics, I suggest you read *Practical Information Architecture: A Hands-On Approach to Structuring Successful Websites* by Eric L. Reiss (2000).

After the participants in the first meeting have signed off on this document, you're ready to go on to the next step, developing a technical requirements document.

From our User Story	Resulting Requirement
...he is returned to the same page. Joe now notices that the name "David Lynch" is clickable. He clicks on it, and it brings up a filmography of David Lynch along with a short biography of the director...	4. In reviews, actor names, movie names, and director names must be links into a search facility of some

Figure 3-1: Requirements document format

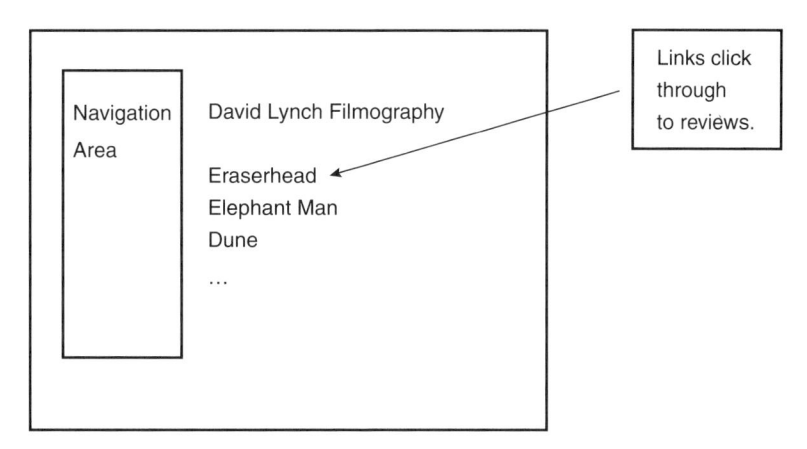

Figure 3-2: Rough interface mockup example

Formal Use Case Analysis with Unified Modeling Language (UML)

The approach I've described in this chapter is loosely based on UML's Use Case Analysis. A more formalized approach to gathering requirements is to use formal Use Case Analysis, which is part of the Unified Modeling Language (UML) lexicon or tool chest. So what is "formal use case analysis"? Use case analysis just means analyzing requirements based on use cases. What UML gives you is strict guidelines and rules for how to document use cases, what a use case is comprised of, and so on. The use cases that I've used in this book (simple declarative sentences) are a rough equivalent to UML's "essential use case." Another kind of use case, called a "real use case," is more concrete and is oriented toward the particular business process you're building. A real use case describes the specific input and output of a process (for example, a person assigned the role of fact checker takes a news article as an input, checks it, and returns a fact-checked news article as an output), the technologies involved (for example, a Web-based interface), the screen flow (for example, the users first see a list of articles to be checked, they choose an article to work on, they see another screen with the full text of the article they chose, and so on), and user interface elements (for example, the user clicks on an article title).

The problem with UML and why many people find it impenetrable, is the wall of terminology that has been built up around it. In this chapter, I've extracted some of the better ideas and presented them in a more humanistic way. I also find that UML often neglects the human elements of requirements gathering in a rigorous attempt to codify. UML often reduces the user to a faceless automaton, a part of a process description, without taking into account the human factors surrounding that user. For instance, the types of services you would build for an end user might differ depending on whether the user is at work or at home. If users are at work, they want quick transactions that accomplish one goal (like "check today's headlines"). If they are at home, they may want other services that draw them into a longer transaction (like "show me all articles about Famke Janssen"). Now think about all the new situations in which you can engage an end user with the growth of mobile devices (in the car, on the train, waiting in line at the bank), and you begin to see why understanding the context and mental state of the user is important.

Having said all that, however, there are enormous benefits to embracing the whole UML system of thought, especially because of UML-based tools, such as Rational Rose. These tools enable you to model your entire application process from requirements capture to code design and implementation. Thus you can look at a method of an object and trace it back to the original use case in the requirements definition that necessitated its existence.

UML is *essential* when you're working on a large application, with many developers working on different parts, especially if those developers are in different locations. However, with small- to medium-sized projects, where you have a development team of, say, five people and the "client" is involved in the process of development, there's a law of diminishing returns with UML. The more effort you put into it, the less value you proportionately get out of it. A better approach with this size project is to pick and choose the pieces of UML that you think are going to help you the most and then apply them appropriately, which is what I've attempted to do here and in the next chapter.

Don't take my word for it. Get a book on UML use case modeling—a really good one is *Use Case Driven Object Modeling with UML: A Practical Approach* by Doug Rosenberg and Kendall Scott (1999). Read it and apply the parts of UML that you think will help the most. If you want to get serious with UML, especially dealing with XML applications, read *Modeling XML Applications with UML: Practical e-Business Applications* by David Carlson (2001).

Quality Assurance

You might think talking about QA this early in the book is putting the cart before the horse. Well, you're wrong. Quality assurance must be a thread that runs through your application from requirements capture, definition, and design, to implementation, and on to deployment. The standard, at least for

Web application development, tends to be "design, develop, test, deploy." You'll notice something peculiar about this methodology: If problems are found in testing (and they always are), no step to fix them is included before the deployment phase. No wonder so much bad code is out there in the world! As humans venture into the universe, we're taking this poorly QAed code with us! A prime example of missing QA was the much-publicized loss of the NASA Mars Climate Orbiter spacecraft in 1999. It spun out of control because part of the software assumed English units and another part assumed metric units. It's *inconceivable* that these code modules were never tested together, but there you go—a half a billion bucks down the drain.

So what can *you* do to make sure you never lose a half a billion smackers? It's actually not that difficult to avoid. The tricky part is thinking about QA and testing at the beginning of the project and developing a comprehensive *test plan* along with your requirements documents and technical specifications. The second tricky part is making sure that you've budgeted enough time and money for testing.

Unit Testing

Unit testing is a testing method that emphasizes testing software at the "unit" level, starting with the simplest units and moving up. Rigorous unit testing should be performed during all stages of development. For example, if you're developing in the Java 2 Enterprise Edition (J2EE) environment (see Chapter 9), Junit is a great framework for unit testing your J2EE building blocks. Check out this link for an informative article that explains Junit: http://developer.java.sun.com/developer/technicalArticles/J2EE/testinfect/.

Integration Testing

Unit testing is great for certifying that software components are working correctly, but eventually you'll need to test that whole subsystems work well when integrated and that the entire system works well as a whole. The way to approach this is to put together a comprehensive testing plan. A great place to start is—you guessed it—your requirements document. Starting with your initial requirements, you can put together a rough testing plan and sample data.

For example, if your original use case is "a user must be able to write an e-mail message," that might translate into several real use cases:

1. User is notified that new e-mail message is waiting for him.
2. User brings up a list of new e-mail messages waiting.
3. User selects an e-mail message to view and reads contents of message.
4. User indicates that he is finished and returns to the list of new messages.

These real use cases might appear in your technical specification document (see the section The Technical Specification Document in this chapter). Each of these use cases can be translated into a test scenario. For example, take the first real use case from the previous list; the test scenario might read like this (depending on your user interface choices):

1. Send a new message to user X.
2. User X should see a notification dialog pop up on her screen with an "OK" button on it.
3. User X should press the "OK" button, and the notification should disappear.

That's the level of granularity you're going for in a test scenario: extremely fine, action-by-action. This approach minimizes confusion on the part of your testers and makes sure different testers consistently test the system. The following are some of the items that might be included in a test plan, depending on the particular project:

- Restatement of the project's purpose.
- Test cases that are built out of granular real use cases (as shown earlier).
- Naming conventions and definitions used in the project, including explanations of all three letter acronyms (TLAs).
- Overall project organization and people/roles involved (including who is responsible for the testing).
- Training needs for testers. What do your testers need to know before they can adequately test the software?

- Testing priorities and focus. Make sure your testers don't get sidetracked testing a part of your application that isn't ready or isn't relevant.
- Test outline: a full description of the test approach by test type, feature, functionality, process, system, module, and so on and so forth.
- Discussion of any specialized software or hardware tools that will be used (such as special testing tools) and in what capacity these are being used.
- Test environment: hardware, operating systems, browser versions, other required software, and so on.
- Problem tracking and resolution tools and processes. How are you going to track problems found? In many projects I've worked on, especially when dealing with a new development environment, we start by building a small bug-tracking application using the same tool with which we'll be building whatever we're building.
- Test metrics to be used. How are you going to grade bugs, and what do those gradations mean?

An important hurdle to get over is the mindset that bugs are bad. If bugs are bad, then people will avoid finding them and not record them in your bug-tracking system. You won't have any bugs in your bug-tracking system, but that doesn't mean there aren't any bugs. This is also a good argument for why developers shouldn't test their own code. You should also think about what your testers are not testing. This is especially important if you have part-time testers, testers who hold other jobs but have agreed to or have been assigned to be testers as part of your project. Set a quota for the number of bugs you want found, and give a reward, even a silly reward like a conference knick-knack, to the tester who finds the most (valid) bugs. Good testing needs to be recognized and rewarded.

The *Software QA/Test Resource Center* (http://www.softwareqatest.com/) is a valuable resource for QA and testing information.

Bugzilla (available at http://www.mozilla.org/bugs/) is an excellent open-source bug- tracking system. It was produced by the folks at the Mozilla open-source browser group to track bugs on their ongoing efforts, but they built it so well that it could be used as a general-purpose tool for bug tracking and resolution.

Mercury Interactive (http://www.mercuryinteractive.com/) provides an evaluation version of their Astra product, which is a pretty comprehensive Web application testing tool. With testing tools like Astra, money sometimes becomes a factor in QA though; remember to budget for these types of tools in your initial plans. Not having good testing tools will definitely cost you more in the long run.

Project Management

Essentially, I've been describing a stripped-down version of a traditional project management approach. It's an approach that I've used with some success, but there's always a "gotcha." As we learned in the story of the *Vasa*, one very big gotcha is scope creep. You start with a list of requirements, develop your product, feel good about it; and, when you finally present it to your users, it's not what they need. So then you have to go back (sometimes to the drawing board) and redo a whole bunch of work. You think your user community is made up of a bunch of morons who don't appreciate all your hard work. Likewise, your user community thinks you're an idiot because you delivered something that wasn't useful to the users. Now they're faced with delays.

I can see some of you nodding your heads, but the problem isn't actually scope creep; it's a disconnect between developer and customer. In response to this disconnect, several software development (or more generalized project management) methods that stress "active user involvement" in the project as it develops have sprung up over the past couple of years. Let's take a look at a couple of them.

Dynamic Systems Development Method (DSDM)

The DSDM consortium promotes its Dynamic Systems Development Method as an alternative to traditional (sometimes called "waterfall") approaches to project management. The DSDM method grew out of more unstructured Rapid Application Development (RAD) methods and stresses involvement, empowerment of team members to make decisions, and short "timeboxed" development efforts, each of which has a definite and useful deliverable. A *timebox* is a fixed measure of time within the project timeline.

DSDM assumes that your project has a fixed delivery date, a timebox in which the project must be completed. This box is then broken into smaller timeboxes, each two to six weeks with assigned prioritized sets of requirements. The prioritization of requirements is key because inevitable delays and setbacks to each timeboxed effort mean that something has to give.

DSDM also attempts to factor scope creep into the equation. It calls for checkpoints throughout the development process at which time changes can be made to scope.

Check out http://www.dsdm.org for the official scoop, white papers, and lots of helpful information on DSDM.

Extreme Programming!

Get extreme! Develop software while bungee jumping out of a balloon over the Grand Canyon! Well, not exactly. Extreme programming is a popular software development method that has sort of had grass roots origins. It may sound out there, but it could actually be the next leap forward in software development.

Extreme programming (or XP as its acolytes refer to it) takes an even more radical approach to software development than DSDM. The XP guys are basically saying that the software development industry created heavy methods for software development but, most of the time, doesn't follow them. XP bills itself as a "lightweight" methodology, built in response to this traditional software development but with strict software engineering practices in mind.

XP doesn't just attempt to manage scope creep; it embraces scope creep. XP is geared toward small projects (with two to ten developers), but it mandates that the team (comprised of developers, customers, and managers, all working elbow-to-elbow) constantly build "spikes" (prototypes) as responses to user requirements. Changing requirements do not necessarily mean that the initial process was flawed. Some of the reasons that requirements change can be good.

- It's difficult to quantify the cost of developing features based purely on hypothesis, in the absence of real development. Once developers

begin to understand the true cost of developing certain features, it might make sense to change the requirements to reduce the project cost.
- Conversely, developers might discover that a particular way of implementing one feature makes other features very easy to implement, justifying the addition of new requirements.
- Competitors may release new products with features that simply must be matched (remember King Adolphus?).
- Discussion with users of similar products (or earlier versions of the same product) may reveal additional information about how features are really used.

There is one hard truth: Requirements changes should always occur as soon as possible (ideally never). One reason why XP emphasizes prototypes is to encourage requirements changes to happen early in the process. Waterfall development often delays requirements changes until after the initial system is fully implemented, which can be very expensive.

One of the more extreme and interesting aspects of XP is the idea that two developers should work together on the same code on the same PC. Programming traditionally has been a solitary task: One developer works slavishly at his PC, generally in a small dark room, while pizzas are periodically slid under the door. XP's "pair programming" challenges this traditional approach by claiming that code can be written at least as efficiently, and with higher quality results, by two developers working at the same PC. One of the developers is typing and thinking tactically, while the other thinks strategically. After considering this approach, you can understand the reasons why it could produce high quality code: Collaboration and interaction can provide a focused environment.

From my experience, the efficacy of this method depends largely on the characteristics of the people involved. Pair programming won't yield better results when the two people working together have personality or communication conflicts, even if they are talented developers. Effective people management is the key.

Another important piece of the XP philosophy is an emphasis on *unit testing*: the testing of individual units of functionality throughout the development process. Unit testing implies that you're writing the code as self-contained modules that fit together, making XP particularly well suited to object-oriented programming, where the emphasis is on self-contained objects.

It's hard to see how King Adolphus's shipbuilders could have applied the principles of XP to their endeavor, but maybe that's the point of the XP approach: Software development methods that treat building software like building a ship may be out of date. Software is an entirely different kind of construct that may be better suited to new and radical design methods.

Visit http://www.extremeprogramming.org to find out about extreme programming, but be warned: XP is not for the faint of heart. A great introductory book on XP is Kent Beck's *Extreme Programming Explained* (1999).

Decide for Yourself

If you think neither DSDM nor XP is for you, check out http://www.ganthead.com, and peruse a whole universe of software development methods. If you can't find what you're looking for here, it probably doesn't exist.

The Technical Specification Document

The next step in project development is to produce a "technical spec," which is a document describing how you're going to implement everything listed in the requirements document. The technical spec has to be separate from the requirements document because the audiences are different. While your functional requirements document is a "public" document that spells things out in nontechnical terms for a nontechnical audience (your users), the technical specification document is to help you with your current and future development efforts. Its audience is technical project managers, architects, and developers. If you do your job in producing the technical spec correctly, your developers will use it as a roadmap as they implement the systems specified in it. Because implementation is often where we learn things while initially writing the technical spec, the spec has to be "living" during the course of implementation.

The technical specification should contain a summary of the problem that the software addresses, a list of the original requirements for the system, as well as your real use cases if you've chosen to model your detailed requirements using real use cases (see the discussion in the section Quality Assurance), the data model diagram, an XML DTD, and a SQL Schema (the last two of which we'll discuss further in the next few chapters), in addition to other technical considerations, such as the development environment, the testing methodologies, the project plan, the separation of duties, and a user interface walk-through.

Summary

The most important points to take away from this chapter are the following:

- Understand who your users (both internal and external) are, and listen to what they have to say while gathering and documenting your requirements.
- Define the problem you are trying to solve before you define the solution. Again, the key is listening and making sure you fully understand the problem you are trying to solve.
- While documenting and analyzing your requirements, be thorough, but don't get so bogged down that you don't see the forest for the trees. Don't get so wrapped up in a single issue that it blinds you to the project as a whole.
- As you pursue the project, know your options, and use the tools (such as project management methodologies) that make sense to you and you are comfortable with.

But don't put all the emphasis on project definition. Don't be afraid to prototype solutions as "solution spikes" (in the XP terminology); show them to your users to gauge their response. Transparency, allowing your customers to see what is happening within the "black box" of the development team, is essential in project management. This kind of participatory approach includes the customer; it breeds respect and "buy in." And there's no greater asset to have when things go wrong, which they inevitably will.

Now that you have an understanding of what you hope to accomplish, it's time to start thinking about your data—what is it going to look like, and how is it going to be structured? We'll get into these questions in Chapter 4.

Chapter 4

Data Modeling

In this chapter, we'll be thinking about data. How do you slice and dice it to meet the needs of your application? We'll start with some simple examples of modeling data and then move on to create a data model for the CyberCinema example from Chapter 3. The focus of this book is on data-oriented application development. Applications that benefit from this approach are those that manage large numbers of records. Applications that might fall into this category are the following:

- Publishing
- Invoice tracking
- Customer service
- Groupware[1]
- Workflow and document management[2]
- Stock trading
- Library automation

---

[1] Software that helps the members of a group, such as a team, communicate or collaborate, such as e-mail or discussions.
[2] A specialized kind of groupware that concentrates on task management.

In all these systems, the applications exist to facilitate access to data or content records.[3] In fact, most computer applications deal with data of one kind or another, from a spreadsheet to a music synthesizer. Computers were invented to perform these types of tasks. In 1890, Herman Hollerith, then working for the U.S. Census Bureau, deployed the first punch card–based system to track immigrants as they passed through the facilities at Ellis Island, New York. Hollerith founded a small company to develop and market this invention. You may be familiar with it; it's called IBM.

Actually, the immigrant-tracking system wasn't the first use of data storage. Joseph Marie Jacquard of France was using punch cards to automate weaving looms in the late eighteenth century (see Figure 4-1). Databases, SQL, and XML represent an evolution, rather than a revolution, in the way we think about and manage large amounts of data. Data-oriented application design is a heritage that stretches back hundreds of years, and it's good to keep this historical context in mind, if only to give you some sense of continuity.

Getting Data-Centric

The first problem to tackle when data modeling is realizing why you need a data model. You might say to yourself, "Forget all this data modeling hokum; I want to get started!" To which I say, "Hold your horses, Tex." Starting data-oriented application development without first understanding what your data is and how you want to use it is like showing up at the O.K. Corral with a jackknife. You're going to get murdered. I can't overstate this: You need data modeling. Without it, you will inevitably fail at whatever you're trying to do, thereby disappointing your user community, your family, and your country. Do you really want your kids to look up at you, their eyes wide with disbelief, and ask, "Why didn't you do the data modeling? Why?" I don't think so.

Data-oriented application design is predicated on the notion that the application and the data are separate and that the data itself is the more important of

---

[3.] A good example of an application that doesn't benefit from this approach would be a real-time application such as the software that runs on your set-top satellite decoder box.

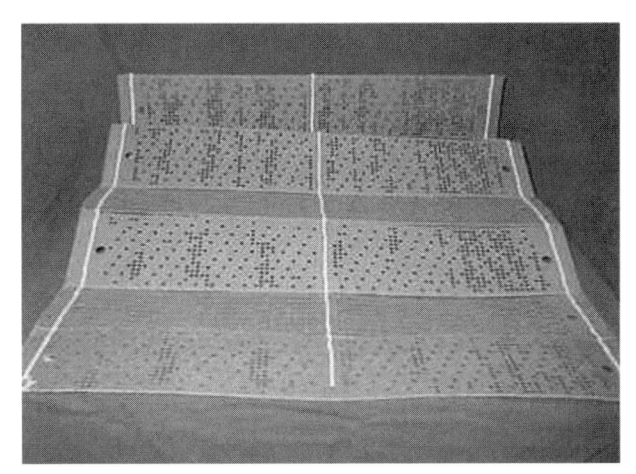

Figure 4-1: Original model of the loom invented Jacquard utilizing punched cards. Photograph by Peter Cook, CompuDudes,® www.compududes.com

the two. For example, imagine you came across a box of the Ellis Island punch cards in your attic. Even if all the original machines for reading and collating these cards had long since rusted, you could build a machine that could read them and store the data in a modern medium. The data on those cards is much more important and durable than any machine or application built to process or manage them.

More recent data storage and management methods sometimes place more importance on the application than on the continuity of the data. Imagine finding a computer hard drive in a pile of junk. What kind of computer was it originally connected to? Assuming you can answer this question and could examine the data on the drive without the original application that produced or managed that data, it would be difficult, if not impossible, to decode.

When designing data-oriented applications using XML, you must learn to separate the data from the application logic. Imagine that in five, ten, or fifty years, someone will build an application different from the one you're currently building, one that will process and use your data. Put yourself in the shoes of that developer. Imagine you found well-formed XML on the discarded hard drive. Even if you didn't have access to the document type definition (DTD) or knowledge of the application, you could make sense of the well-formed XML.

Data-oriented application architects and developers have an obligation to the future. That obligation is to build their data models in an application-independent fashion. At the risk of mixing my metaphors even more, a good data model is a road map that will keep you on the straight and narrow. The first step down the road to modeled data is to ask, "What is my data?" This question, like many aspects of application design and development, is deceptively simple.

Show Me the Data!

Let's say we're building a simple e-mail system. A dumbed-down set of requirements, perfect for this overly simplistic example, might be expressed in use cases (see Chapter 2 for a discussion of use cases), such as the following:

- A user must be able to write an e-mail message.
- A user must be able to send e-mail to another user.
- A user must be able to read e-mail sent to him from another user.
- An e-mail will consist of a subject line and a message body.

These use cases are a way of expressing requirements. Consider an example of an e-mail message. Unless you've been under a rock for the past 15 years, you know that an e-mail message consists of the following:

- **To:** field
- **From:** field
- **Subject:** field
- Message **body**

In reality, of course, an e-mail message contains other fields that the user might never see, but we'll limit our discussion to these four fields. Each of these fields has different properties. The To: and From: fields must contain valid e-mail addresses. The Subject: field must contain a short line of text, and the body of the message can contain many paragraphs of text.

I've just described a simple data model for e-mail messages. Notice I haven't mentioned data types or string lengths, nor have I defined "e-mail address." Data models are meant to be *abstract* representations. Stay away from concrete definitions such as "The subject is stored as a Unicode string and can be up to 255 characters long."

The reason we want to keep the data model abstract is that we're going to be defining these entities in multiple frameworks later. Something that's represented by a string data type in our Java code, for instance, might be represented by a `varchar` data type in our database and as CDATA in our XML DTD. We'll get into some of that later in Chapters 5 and 6, but for now, let's keep things abstract. At this point, you ask the second most important question (see the following section).

What Do You Hope to Accomplish?

Asking what you hope to accomplish brings reality into the picture: What are the requirements of the system you're developing? Let's look back at the requirements use cases:

- A user must be able to write an e-mail message.
- A user must be able to send e-mail to another user.
- A user must be able to read e-mail sent to him from another user.
- An e-mail will consist of a subject line and a message body.

In examining our requirements, we've discovered that we actually have another element to contend with—users. If our data model is to be of any use in application design, it must encompass users as well as e-mail messages themselves, and it must describe the relationship between users and e-mail messages. This relationship is implicit in the preceding requirements: Users write and read e-mail messages.

Now we're back to our original questions: What is the data? What data do we want to track about our users? For simplicity's sake, we'll say that users consist of user names, full names, and passwords (because we don't want our users reading each other's mail, unless you're into that kind of thing).

Making It Visual: Entity Relationship Diagrams

Data modeling visualization techniques are many and varied, and it's not within the scope of this book to discuss all of them. As discussed previously—see the sidebar in Chapter 3, Formal Use Case Analysis with Unified Modeling Language (UML)—UML provides a useful set of tools for requirements capture and use case analysis. It also provides a diagrammatic structure and an approach to data modeling. The approach I've found most useful, and the one I've taken in this book, is to use a simplified version of UML.

In Figure 4-2, we see how we can begin to model our e-mail system and users, which can be referred to as *user entities*. A box represents each entity. The entity name is at the top of the box, and the attributes of that entity are listed below the entity name. The line between the two boxes indicates that some kind of relationship exists between the two entities. Again, notice that this data model is abstract, in that we're not defining data types or the nature of the relationship.

Roll Film: Back to CyberCinema

In the previous chapter, we built a sample requirements document for a proposed CyberCinema movie review Web site. In the case of CyberCinema, the answer to the question "What is the data?" seems quite simple—movie reviews. Application designers have to be suspicious by nature, and this answer is suspiciously simple. Delving into this answer a little deeper, we can ask, "What are movie reviews?" Movie reviews essentially are articles, and articles consist of paragraphs of written text. The subject matter is movies. Movie reviews are written *by* someone, so there's author information as well. A data model begins to take shape, as shown in Figure 4-3.

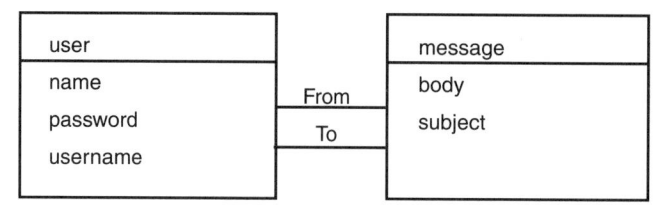

Figure 4-2: Data modeling diagram for e-mail system

Great, we're finished. Just to be sure, though, let's go back to our requirements document and double-check that we've covered all the use cases in our requirements.

1. Reviewers must be able to write reviews.
2. Reviews can contain normal text features such as bold, italic, and underline.
3. Reviews can include headings to delineate one section of a review from another.
4. In reviews, actor names, movie names, and director names must be links to a search facility of some kind.
5. Reviews can contain links to other reviews.
6. Reviews can contain links to outside URLs.
7. Reviews must be searchable by movie.
8. Reviews must be searchable by director.
9. Reviews must be searchable by actor.
10. Reviews must be searchable by reviewer.
11. Movies must be searchable by director.
12. Movies must be searchable by actor.

We won't able to meet these requirements with our conceived data model. For example, we're not addressing directors, actors, or reviewers in the data model, so we won't be able to satisfy requirements 8–12. If we're going to be able to look up movie reviews reliably by actor, director, and reviewer, and movies by actor and director, we must include these elements in our model. By creating separate elements in our data model (and subsequently, our database schema, as we'll see in Chapter 6), the database will be able to look up information based on these items.

MovieReview
Author
Movie
Body of Review

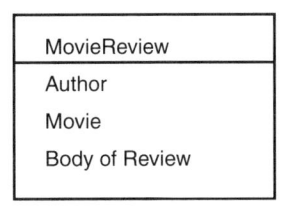

Figure 4-3: First cut of CyberCinema data model diagram

Normalization Equals Power: Defining Relationships

If you rely on the title of a movie to uniquely identify it in your data model, how are you going to differentiate *The Parent Trap* with Haley Mills from *The Parent Trap* with Dennis Quaid? If you rely on names to uniquely identify actors, how is your system going to know that Robin Wright is the same person as Robin Wright Penn? The only way to reliably track all these different types of data is to separate them into different logical entities (such as directors, actors, and reviewers).

Thus, we now have several "entities" that we wish to manage in our fledgling system: movie reviews, movies, review authors, actors, and directors. Let's redraw our data model (see Figure 4-4) and take a look at what we're working with.

Keep It Simple: No Really, I Mean It

When looking at the data model in Figure 4-4, if you're thinking "Something looks very similar between actor, director, and reviewer," great! Now you're starting to think like a data architect. You've noticed that the only difference between the actor, director, and reviewer entities is the name of the entity. By

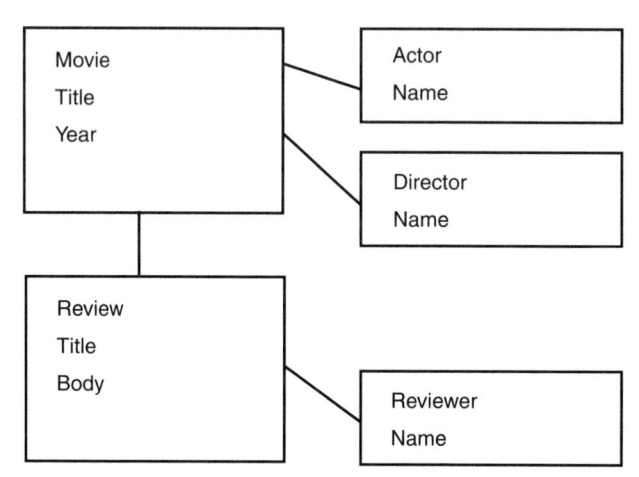

Figure 4-4: Redrawn CyberCinema data model diagram, including actors, directors, and reviewers

collapsing these three entities into one all-encompassing "person" entity, we can greatly simplify this model, while allowing it to retain its power.

If we were doing an object-oriented design at this stage, we might create a "person" superclass and make "actor," "director," and "reviewer" subclasses of this "person" class. When you get to the stage where you actually start writing application code, you may, in fact, want to do this. Remember that this is data-oriented application design. The idea is to think through the data model first, without considering implementation specifics. Thinking in terms of superclasses and subclasses is an important part of application design, but we want to keep such application-centric thinking out of our abstract data model. Notice we're also not talking explicitly about the use of XML at this point; that also comes later, after the abstract design is complete.

So, keeping the abstract mantra in mind, we'll reduce our actor, director, and reviewer entities into one "person" entity (see Figure 4-5).

Even though the data model in Figure 4-5 has one person entity where before we had three entities (actor, director, and reviewer), we've kept three relationships in our diagram, represented by the lines bridging the three entities (Movie, Review, and Person).

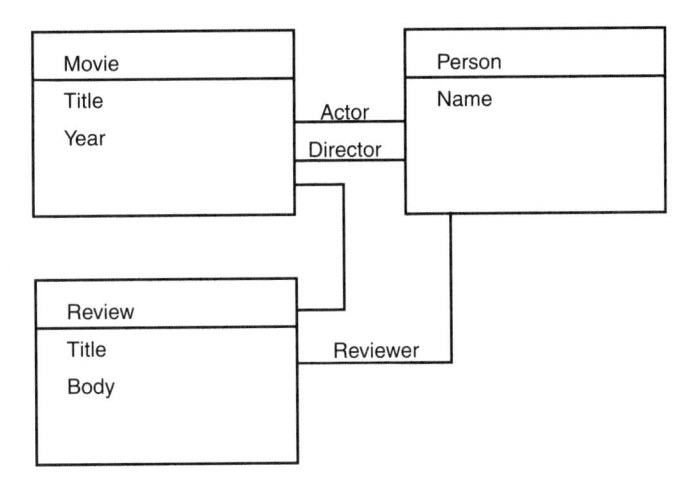

Figure 4-5: Simplified CyberCinema data model

We know that people act in and direct movies and that people also author reviews (using *author* as a verb).

Getting Complex: Many-to-One and Many-to-Many Relationships

In order for our reviewers to be able to write more than one review, we must redefine the relationship between review and reviewer as a many-to-one relationship. Luckily, UML provides a simple notation for doing so (see Figure 4-6).

In Figure 4-6, the *n* and *1* represent the nature of the relationship between reviewer and review. A single reviewer (*1*) can write any number of reviews (*n*). Of course, multiple reviewers can collaborate on the same review, but with this realization, the data modelers are tempted to say, "Enough is enough! No! One reviewer per review, and that's it!"

Their resistance is because these rather callous modelers no doubt have built such systems before, and they are envisioning a relational table structure that could accommodate multiple authors per review—and they're cringing. They're cringing with good reason. This is when the requirements for a system start to balloon, sending even the most mild-mannered engineers into apoplectic fits. Calm down. Go to your happy place. Remember, we're not dealing with specific implementation issues when modeling data.

Returning to our requirements document, we may see that, in fact, multiple reviewers *can* collaborate on a review. It pays to focus on the data model itself here, leaving aside all thoughts related to implementation. We can worry about implementation later.

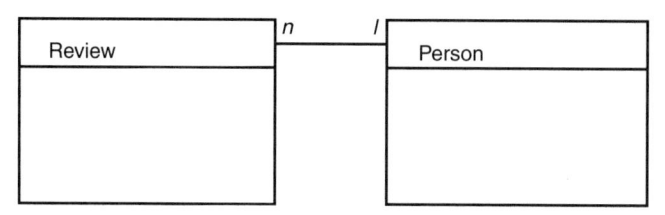

Figure 4-6: A many-to-one relationship

For each relationship we've defined, we now must ask the question: Is this a *one-to-one* relationship, a *one-to-many* relationship, or a *many-to-many* relationship? Let's step through each relationship.

- Can a review be written by more than one reviewer? Yes
- Can a reviewer write more than one review? Yes
- *Thus reviewer to review is a many-to-many relationship.*
- Can a movie have more than one actor? Unless the actor is Spalding Grey, yes, and the same goes for director.
- Can an actor be in more than one movie? Unfortunately, in some cases, yes.
- *Thus actor to movie is a many-to-many relationship.*
- Can a review be about more than one movie? Yes.
- Can a movie be reviewed more than once? Undoubtedly.
- *Thus movie to review is a many-to-many relationship.*

It's beginning to look like our data model consists mostly of many-to-many relationships between entities. Our new diagram is shown in Figure 4-7.

Another Layer of Complexity: Adding Media

If you have been paying attention, you may have noticed that we didn't correctly list all the requirements for our CyberCinema Web site. We left out one requirement: that reviews can include photographs or other media (such as video or sound clips). One approach to modeling this layer of complexity might be to leave media out of your data model entirely. The reasoning might go something like this:

> Well, this is for a Web site, so we can embed the images or media into the articles using HTML tags while the actual files can sit on disk somewhere. According to the requirements document, we're never going to search for or look up the reviews based on media, so we're good to go with the previously conceived data model.

Unfortunately, using this reasoning, you've just lost the ability to manage your media. For example, consider that the publishers of the site, after CyberCin-

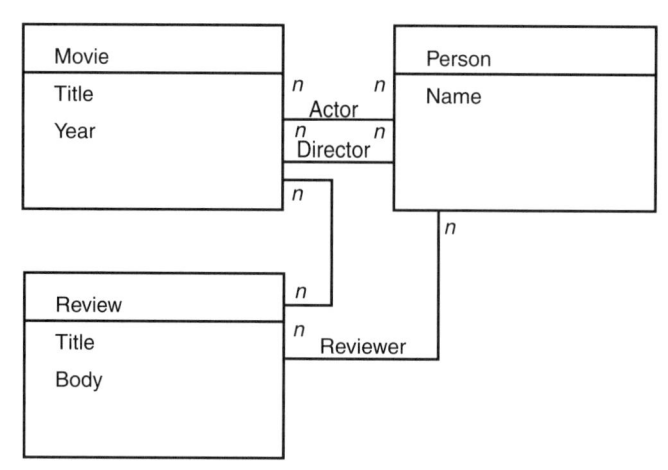

```
            Movie                        Person
                         n         n
            Title                        Name
                              Actor
            Year              n       n
                              Director

                               n
                                             n
            Review
                              n
            Title
                                  Reviewer
            Body
```

Figure 4-7: CyberCinema data modeling diagram with relationships

ema is launched, could decide they want the search results screens to display next to review titles icons, indicating whether the review contains images, a video clip, or a sound clip. If you use the previous reasoning on which to base your data model, you're in serious trouble.

The next instinct of a novice data modeler is usually to allow graphics to be part of the data model, but allow only one piece of media per review. That will keep everyone happy and the data model simple. Using this reasoning, you're imposing an artificial constraint on your review authors, based only on your prior experience that a one-to-one relationship is easier to implement than a many-to-many relationship. Although it's a valid reason and follows the "keep it simple" mantra, such reasoning is another case of falling into the trap of implementation-specific thinking.

For the purposes of our abstract data model, all we need to know is that media entities (for simplicity's sake, we'll wrap them into one entity) can be embedded in reviews and have a many-to-many relationship with reviews. A new data model diagram incorporating these changes is shown in Figure 4-8.

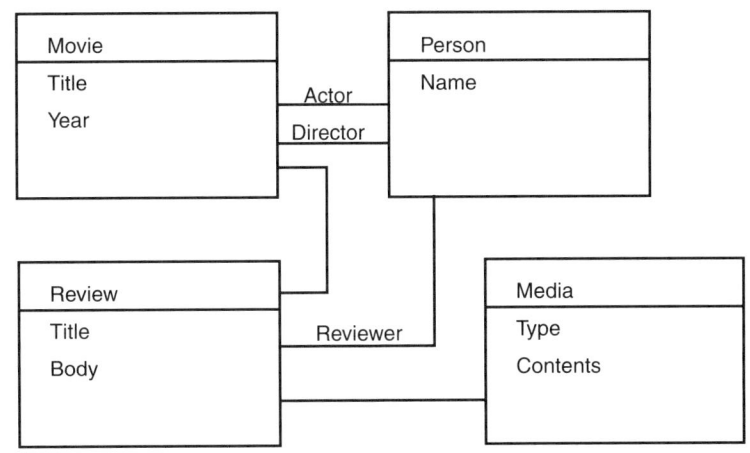

Figure 4-8: Revised CyberCinema data model diagram, incorporating new "media" entity

Summary

The most important points you should learn from this chapter are to keep your data modeling abstract and (as much as possible) application-independent. Obviously, you can't anticipate every possible future requirement for the data your application will manage, but try to be forward-thinking when building this abstract model. Incorporate features in your data model to support application features that aren't implemented yet. Remember that it's easier to change your application code than it is to change your data model—that's why you do the data model first.

Now that we've got a workable abstract model of our data, we're ready to begin the rest of our infrastructure design. Following the traditional relational development model, we would now start coding SQL table CREATE statements. In the object-oriented universe, we would flesh out our entities as objects and determine what methods we want to build into each one.

In our case, because we're building an XML application, we'll move first to designing our XML documents.

Chapter 5

XML Design

In which we dig up a rock and discover the secrets of time.

The beauty of XML is its flexibility. It's a toolkit with which you build your own markup language to meet your particular needs exactly, because *you* design it.

The focus of this chapter is on building an XML DTD (document type definition). However, the DTD is only one way to build an XML design. For example, an XML Schema, which is discussed in Chapter 7, and XDR (XML Data–Reduced), which is discussed in Chapter 8, are other means of creating an XML design used in different contexts. The principles discussed in this chapter can be applied to these other methods as well.

It's worthwhile to focus on DTDs because the DTD is the most essential form of XML design. Understanding DTDs, which date back to SGML days, gives you insight into how XML works, so even if you don't intend to build a DTD, read on.

We'll start our XML design by creating dummy XML instances, which give a good idea of what our real XML instances are going to look like, the elements we'll need, and the attributes those elements should have. Then we'll put together a DTD based on these dummy instances, fleshing it out to take into account possibilities we may not have put into the dummy instances. At the end of this process, we'll have a DTD (for the complete DTD for the CyberCinema example, see the Appendix) and some sample XML files that can be used as test files during the subsequent development process.

Carving Your Rosetta Stone

In the late eighteenth century archeologists had a problem. They found a lot of tablets written in a script, Egyptian hieroglyphs, they couldn't decipher. It was only after French soldiers in Napoleon's army unearthed a large stone tablet in 1799 that archaeologists were able to make a breakthrough in deciphering the script. On the stone was written a decree, inscribed in Egyptian hieroglyphics, Greek, and demotic characters (the basis of a later Egyptian script). English and French archeologists eventually were able to "crack" the code of Egyptian hieroglyphs through their knowledge of Greek, vastly enlarging the amount of material that fifth-grade social studies teachers have to teach.

The XML application designer's equivalent to a Rosetta stone is the XML DTD. A DTD, or document type definition, describes how your individual XML instances are constructed. A DTD describes which XML elements are allowed, their attributes, and how they fit together to form a *valid* piece of XML.

Figure 5-1: The Rosetta Stone

> ### Elements and Attributes
>
> When structuring data, we first separate it into two classes: *elements* and *attributes* of elements. These terms have several different meanings, depending on the context. Each has a specific definition within the XML and the SQL lexicons. For the purposes of this book, I mostly use the XML meanings of elements and attributes. As the following illustrates (from an XML example taken from Chapter 1), the element is the book, while the attribute is the ISBN)
>
> Element
> ```
> <book isbn = "0987-2343">Odyssey</book>
> ```
> Attribute

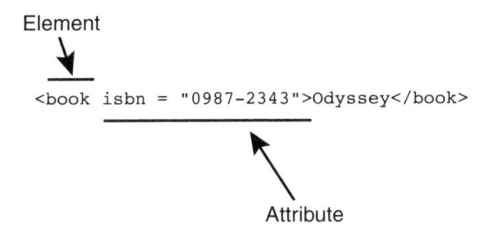

Where Is the DTD Used?

Because the DTD is a machine-readable document, it is part of your finished system, enforcing the rules set forth in it and assisting different application components in dealing with your XML instances. For example, an application environment might use a DTD to create object classes based on the elements in its DTD. Any text editor or word processor can be used to edit XML documents, but *structured* XML editors use the DTD to enforce compliance at the input level, restricting authors from using invalid XML codes. Likewise, your application can "validate" individual XML instances against the DTD to ensure that they conform. This is especially important when you're accepting XML from external sources (such as other businesses) or when your XML is being authored in one system and delivered through another system (as often happens in the realm of content management). In these types of situations, you'll want to validate your XML against the DTD before processing it further.

> ### Note
>
> In XML-land, an *instance* is a word for a self-contained bit of XML that is well formed, that is, it conforms to XML's syntax rules (such as the tag nesting structure) and therefore is legal XML. An instance is usually the same as a document,

although this isn't always the case. For example, a single text file document might be made up of many XML instances (you might concatenate several XML instances together into a single file to transfer the file between systems). Readers familiar with object-oriented terminology should find nothing odd about the use of the term *instance* for an XML document. Essentially, a DTD is a *class*, and an XML document is an *instance* of that class.

When to Use XML and When Not to Use It

In Chapter 4, you braved the waters of abstract data modeling, so now it's time to get concrete. Building your XML DTD is the next step in data-oriented application design.

The first question you must ask, while looking at your abstract data model diagram from Chapter 4 (see Figure 4-7) is "Where doesn't XML fit?" Identify the parts of your data model that make more sense as purely relational entities. Such parts usually are supporting data, such as key words and author names. For example, in CyberCinema there's no reason to list valid reviewers in an XML file. The reviewers and details about them (for example, names and e-mail addresses) can be stored in a relational table. The reviews themselves are best stored as XML.

Think Like an Archeologist

Put yourself in the mindset of an archeologist in the future, leafing through a collection of your XML instances. If you're thinking, "I am not writing this application for future archeologists," you're missing the point. The Rosetta stone wasn't created for the benefit of future archeologists; it was created for the dissemination of information in its own time. By carefully building and documenting the DTD, you make your data more useful not only for today but also in the future.

Suppose you're an archeologist who came across a collection of XML instances. Consider what information must be in those instances in order for you to reconstruct the application that created them—to crack the code of this found data. Let's use as an example the simple e-mail application we built a data model for in Chapter 4. Your first step should be to "roughout" an XML vocabulary by creating some XML instances. This helps you understand the tagging structure before jumping headfirst into DTD design. Create a few of these dummy files. They're not intended to be used by your programs; they're just a tool to help you visualize what the XML files will look like and how they need to be structured. A first stab at an XML instance for this application might look like the following:

```
<E-MAIL>
<FROM>Dan Appelquist</FROM>
<TO>Bill Gates</TO>
<SUBJECT>I Like Windows</SUBJECT>
<BODY>Thanks for all the hard work.</BODY>
</E-MAIL>
```

This XML instance makes it easy for us to distinguish the From: field from the To: field and so on, but it doesn't help us construct an application in conjunction with a relational database.

We're designing this XML to work hand-in-hand with a relational database. In particular, we have to understand where numerical ID numbers come into play. Relational database schemas use numerical ID numbers in order to identify items uniquely and to preserve cross-references. Most of these ID numbers are generated as they are needed: When you insert a new row into a table, you first generate a new ID number. Depending on how your database works, ID number generation may be an automatic feature; it may involve setting up a database sequence, a feature of a database that generates consecutive unique numbers. Or it could be a number generated somewhere in the application and inserted into the database. In any case, it is a number that's unique at least to a particular set of items (for example, e-mail messages in our simple e-mail application).

For our e-mail application, if we assume that ID numbers are going to be assigned to each e-mail message, those numbers have to be reflected in the XML instance as well, so that we know which XML instances match up with which rows in our relational database. We do that by adding an ID attribute to the E-MAIL element we've created. Note that the name "ID" doesn't have any special meaning in XML instances; I simply decided to call it that. Because users are another item that will be stored in the relational database, we'll also include an ID field in our TO and FROM elements. Our message subject and body don't need unique IDs because they are unique to the message itself. Now have the following:

```
<E-MAIL ID="1">
<FROM ID="2">Dan Appelquist</FROM>
<TO ID="3">Bill Gates</TO>
<SUBJECT>I Like Windows</SUBJECT>
<BODY>Thanks for all the hard work.</BODY>
</E-MAIL>
```

Again, adopting the perspective of an archeologist in the future, suppose you came across thousands of XML instances in the preceding format. You could reconstruct not only a database of messages but also a database of all users who were part of this system. You could reconstruct entire conversations. If a user changed his or her name sometime during the operational period of the system, you wouldn't care because you'd be able to identify users by their unique IDs. In this manner, XML makes it possible for you to "future-proof" your documents.

Oh, by the way, if you happen not to be a future archeologist, but a system administrator or database administrator or DBA, frantically trying to reconstruct a database after a system crash, you may be thankful that the DTD was well designed. Future-proofing also means disaster-proofing your data.

Building a DTD

The next step in XML design is to build a DTD based on the rough instance we worked out for the previous example. A DTD, in its simplest form, contains a declaration of every element you want to use in your XML instances. Examining the XML instance we defined in the previous section, the elements are

- E-MAIL
- FROM

- TO
- SUBJECT
- BODY

Each of these elements must be defined within the DTD using an "ELEMENT" keyword, such as:

```
<!ELEMENT E-MAIL (FROM, TO, SUBJECT, BODY)>
<!ELEMENT FROM (#CDATA)*>
<!ELEMENT TO (#CDATA)*>
<!ELEMENT SUBJECT (#CDATA)*>
<!ELEMENT BODY (#CDATA)*>
```

Each of the preceding lines declares an element that legally can be part of our XML instances. Each declaration has two parts: the element name, such as FROM, and its *content model*, which defines what the element can contain. Notice what's going on in the declaration for the E-MAIL element: We've defined its content model very rigidly. It *must* contain a FROM element, followed by a TO element, followed by a SUBJECT element, followed by a BODY element. Any other order is illegal under this content model. The content models of the FROM, TO, SUBJECT, and BODY elements, however, are defined with the cryptic #CDATA, which stands for "character data" and really just means "character text" such as the text of this sentence. This means that the content model of these items can be any character text, but other XML elements or entities are not allowed. If you want to include elements or entities in your character data, you use the designation content model #PCDATA (which stands for parseable character data).

XML Character Entities

What happens if the text within your XML instance needs to include a character like "<" (the "less than" symbol)? Because "<" has a special meaning in XML, if you just stick it in the middle of a sentence, you're going to get a big fat parsing error when you try to use this XML instance. The answer is to use XML entity references in place of these characters. Entity references start with an ampersand (&), followed by a code and then a semicolon. For instance, the XML standard entity reference for < is <. Of course, this makes & into a reserved symbol as well, requiring its own entity reference (&). XML defines a set of standard entity references for these and other special characters, but you can also define your own entity references.

For example, if your XML instances were music reviews about Prince albums released after 1993, you might want to define a new entity for that little squiggly ankh-thingy (&theartist;).

Your application can then substitute a suitable graphic image when representing the article to a reader. I've used this approach with Greek letters (for example, α for α) and other mathematical symbols with great success.

You define which character entities you want to be legal in your XML at the top of your DTD with an external reference like:

```
<!ENTITY % HTMLlat1 PUBLIC
    "-//W3C//ENTITIES Latin1//EN//HTML"
    "HTMLlat1.ent">
%HTMLlat1;
```

This defines that all of the character entities in the "Latin 1" set are now part of your DTD. These include £ (£), ½ (½) and Ö (Ö) for documents about heavy metal bands).

Full definitions of these predefined entity sets are available from the W3C site as part of the definition of HTML (www.w3.org/MarkUp/).

Entities can also be used to build a shorthand for a complex content model for use in a DTD. For instance, if you wanted your e-mail subject and body to be able to contain characters, entities, and the elements <i> and <b> (for italic and bold), you might define an entity in your DTD like this:

```
<!ENTITY % text "(#PCDATA | i | b)*">
```

Then you would define the content models for your BODY and SUBJECT elements like this:

```
<!ELEMENT SUBJECT &text;>
<!ELEMENT BODY &text;>
```

In the full DTD for CyberCinema in the Appendix there are more examples of this use of entities.

Now that we've defined our elements and how they fit together (their content models), we need to define each element's attributes.

Reexamining our sample instance, we find that our only attributes are ID numbers, inside the E-MAIL, TO, and FROM elements. Each element must have its own attribute list declaration (using the ATTLIST keyword), like so:

```
<!ATTLIST E-MAIL      ID     NMTOKEN    #REQUIRED>
<!ATTLIST FROM        ID     NMTOKEN    #REQUIRED>
<!ATTLIST TO          ID     NMTOKEN    #REQUIRED>
```

Each attribute declaration consists first of an identifier associating it with a specific element (in this case, E-MAIL, FROM, and TO), the attribute's name (ID), and its type (NMTOKEN, which is a reserved type set aside for tokens consisting of letters or numbers). Adding the #REQUIRED reserved word to each declaration means that every element of this type *must* have a specified ID number. An instance of an e-mail where the FROM field, for example, doesn't have an ID number is not valid according to our DTD and would fail a validation test against the DTD.

The ordering of these declarations isn't important, but an attribute list declaration for an element should occur after the declaration of the element itself in the DTD. This keeps the DTD readable and keeps you sane.

Commenting Code

Comments (that is, nonfunctional, nonparseable bits of text included to provide information to the reader) within a DTD (and within XML documents in general) are denoted using the following syntax:

```
<!-- This is a comment -->
```

Commenting your DTD is just as crucial as commenting a piece of application code, especially if you expect someone else to be able to decipher it. Remember that future archeologist?

The following is the entire DTD for our simple e-mail system:

```
<!-- This is the DTD for our simple e-mail system  -->
<!-- An e-mail message must contain from, to, subject, and body fields,
     in that order  -->
<!ELEMENT E-MAIL (FROM, TO, SUBJECT, BODY)>
<!-- The from, to, subject, and body fields contain only character
     data  -->
<!ELEMENT FROM (#CDATA)*>
<!ELEMENT TO (#CDATA)*>
<!ELEMENT SUBJECT (#CDATA)*>
<!ELEMENT BODY (#CDATA)*>
<!-- The e-mail message itself is identified by a numerical ID  -->
<!ATTLIST E-MAIL   ID    NMTOKEN    #REQUIRED>
<!-- The from and to fields are identified by numerical IDs which
     reference database id numbers for these users. -->
<!ATTLIST FROM     ID    NMTOKEN    #REQUIRED>
<!ATTLIST TO       ID    NMTOKEN    #REQUIRED>
```

CyberCinema: The Rosetta Stone Meets the Web

Let's consider our previous example of the CyberCinema Web site. The considerations here are a bit more complex, but the same basic process applies: Start by roughing out some XML instances and then move on to DTD design. The complexity is introduced when we consider our user population and how users are going to interact with the XML instances in the system.

Let's start by listing a few assumptions, derived from our requirements document (see Chapter 3) and subsequent data model (see Chapter 4):

1. For CyberCinema, each review is represented by a single XML instance.
2. Each review is stored in a database.
3. In this database, we also track movies, review authors, actors, and directors.
4. Review authors can refer to specific movies, actors, and directors in the text of their articles, and those references can be hyperlinks (for example, to a filmography of a particular actor or director).

5. The primary delivery platform for CyberCinema movie reviews is the Web, although the reviews also are syndicated to other sites, to information retrieval services, and potentially to print media.

The first three requirements are fairly straightforward, but with requirements 4 and 5, things start to get hairy. Splitting the problem into two domains makes sense at this point. The two domains are recordlike data and narrativelike data. XML is good for both domains, but understanding the difference is extremely important to effective DTD design.

Recordlike data is anything that sounds like it would feel at home in a traditional relational schema, for instance, author information, a headline, or the title of the movie the review is about.

Narrativelike data, generally speaking, is anything where order is meaningful. For example, if you rearranged the words in this sentence, as follows, the meaning of the sentence is lost:

> Sentence, if for the in, as example, rearranged the meaning follows you of the is sentence words lost this.

However, as noted previously, if you rearrange the declarations in our e-mail DTD, they still form a valid DTD declaration. The DTD declaration is recordlike, whereas the sentence is narrativelike. The term *narrative-like* may be a bit confusing because we're still talking about all kinds of data (words, images, links, formatting, and so on), not just narrative data in its strictest sense.

So that your documents make sense, I suggest you separate them into a head section and a body section. The head section should contain recordlike information, and the body section should contain narrativelike information. This is not to say that there is no gray area between recordlike and narrativelike information. The rule of thumb is that the main part of a document that usually renders as one block of text is the body; anything else goes in the head.

Given that we're separating our movie reviews into head and body information, a skeleton structure for an instance of a review looks like this:

```
<?xml version="1.0">
<CYBERCINEMA_REVIEW ID="123">
```

```
<HEAD>
    <!-- Header information goes here -->
</HEAD>
<BODY>
    <!-- Body information goes here -->
</BODY>
</CYBERCINEMA_REVIEW>
```

A Note on White Space

All XML instances presented here are formatted for readability, so that white space (carriage returns, tabs, or spaces) appears between tags. In XML, white space is meaningful, which can be tricky. What this means is that if you have a space between the end of one tag and the start of another, an XML parser will view that space as a meaningful part of your document. If you want to be able to have white space in your document, you need to account for it in the content model of your elements. I think it's better to ensure that your XML instances don't contain any white space between tags, except where it is meaningful to the document itself. Depending on what authoring environment your user population employs, white space may be taken care of for you. In the systems I've built, special routines have always been needed for dealing with white space, or the lack thereof, in XML instances on their way in and out of the system. Your XML editing environment should take care of presenting the XML instances in a friendly way (not all on one line), so you really shouldn't need to have extra white space characters in the instances themselves.

The Head

We've defined the head of our XML instance as containing recordlike information. Looking back at our requirements for CyberCinema, we see that the following recordlike pieces of information are associated with each review:

- Author
- Headline
- Summary or abstract of the review

- Date the review was "published" (that is, the date the review was released, not necessarily the date it was created or last modified, so you may also want to track the *create* date and the *last modified* date)
- Movie being reviewed

Dates

Throughout this book, when I refer to *dates* or *timestamps*, I'm talking about "date and time," as in an exact measurement of the date and time. We'll get into how exact later (see the sidebar A Brief History of Time later in this chapter).

Remember, information about actors and directors and about the graphics embedded in reviews belongs in the body not in the head of the review. The body is perfectly capable of storing structured information; it isn't an unstructured blob that is included for display purposes only.

Singular Versus Plural: Putting Together Blocks

One important question to ask yourself about each piece of information you put in the head of the instance is: Is it plural or singular? We've stated that reviews can have more than one author, so author information is plural. A review shouldn't have multiple headlines or abstracts, so the headline and abstract are singular. An article can't be created twice or published for the first time twice, so these events are singular. They happen only once, so the date stamps for them are also singular. Although an article can be modified more than once, in this example we're tracking only the time the article was last modified.

Organizing plural elements within blocks is a convenient way to group them together and set them apart from the other elements within the head, like organizing files in file folders. Let's continue with our example of movie reviews. The head consists of a single "author block," which contains all author information, and then a set of singular items: REVIEWED, HEADLINE, ABSTRACT, CREATE_DATE, LASTMOD_DATE, and PUBLISH_DATE. By using a single author block to store all of the author information, you also make it easier to extract this information from the XML later on because extracting it requires only one operation: finding and retrieving the author block. The alternative would be to find and retrieve each author entry separately.

The head of our document is starting to take shape. Building on the skeleton we constructed previously, we have a good idea of what the head looks like:

```xml
<?xml version="1.0">
<CYBERCINEMA_REVIEW ID="123">
    <HEAD>
        <!-- Header information goes here -->
        <AUTHOR_BLOCK>
            <AUTHOR ID="123">Daniel Appelquist</AUTHOR>
        </AUTHOR_BLOCK>
        <REVIEWED ID="3827">Gone With the Wind</REVIEWED>
        <HEADLINE>Classic Film Still Fresh</HEADLINE>
        <ABSTRACT>This film is often thought of as the best example of classic...</ABSTRACT>
        <CREATE_DATE DATE="2000-05-17T17:10:00,0"/>
        <LASTMOD_DATE DATE="2000-05-17T18:12:00,0"/>
        <PUBLISH_DATE DATE="2000-05-17T19:27:00,0"/>
    </HEAD>
    <BODY>
        <!-- Body information goes here -->
    </BODY>
</CYBERCINEMA_REVIEW>
```

You'll notice that the date stamp elements in the HEAD element look a little funny—their tags end with a forward slash, as in `<PUBLISH_DATE DATE=""/>`. This forward slash at the end of a tag is the notation for an *empty* element. It is one of the main differences between XML and the markup languages that have come before it (such as HTML). It's a shorthand way of using an opening tag `<PUBLISH_DATE DATE="">` and a closing tag`</PUBLISH_DATE>` next to each other. In fact, these two bits of code (the single XML date tag that ends with the forward slash and the pair of opening and closing tags) are functionally identical; `<PUBLISH_DATE DATE=""/>` is just a more convenient and cleaner way to represent elements that don't have contents (such as these date stamps, which have only attributes).

A Brief History of Time

As in the previous example, when a date and/or time must be specified in an element (as in the `<PUBLISH_DATE>` element), a good way to do it is to use the following format:

```
CCYY-MM-DDThh:mm:ss,s
```

Each of the letters in the preceding example is a placeholder for a digit. `CCYY` indicates century and then year, `MM` is the month, and `DD` is the day of the month. `T` is a literal character, `hh` is the hour of the day (in 24-hour time), `mm` is the minutes of the hour, and `ss` is the seconds in the minute. The final `s` represents tenths of a second—useful when you *really* need to be precise. This format is the Extended Format of calendar date and local time of day as described by the International Standards Organization (in ISO8601, section 5.4.1, clause a). Because the ISO has provided a standard way to represent date/time in your XML instances, *don't reinvent the wheel*. Use this format and convert dates in and out of it for all the other date formats you need (for instance, for display purposes in another format such as May 17, 1997 or 1997-05-17 or to insert a date into a date field in a database).

For example, the formatted string for May 17, 1997, at 17:00 is

```
1997-05-17T17:00:00,0
```

To access the complete ISO standard in PDF form (you will be amazed at how much can be written on the topic of "What time is it?"), check http://www.iso.ch/markete/8601.pdf.

To complicate things a bit more, whenever you give something a timestamp, you have to consider the issue of time zones. This issue is especially important for systems that operate over the Internet because your XML instances frequently will cross time zones. One approach, which I favor, is to represent all timestamps in GMT (Greenwich mean time). Make sure that every time you represent a timestamp, you're translating it to the current time zone. (You also have to make allowances for daylight savings time, which requires care because daylight savings time changes at different times depending on where on earth you are.) All other time zones are annotated in relation to GMT (for example, U.S. eastern standard time is GMT-5) so representing timestamps in GMT is quite natural and not at all a throwback to a bygone era of the British empire.

Of course, you could reject using GMT and use Swatch's "Internet-Time" (http://www.swatch.com/). But people might think you're on hallucinogenic drugs, so I would shy away from it if I were you.

A DTD fragment for the previous DTD follows:

```
<!ELEMENT HEAD (AUTHOR_BLOCK, REVIEWED, HEADLINE, ABSTRACT, CREATE_DATE,
LASTMOD_DATE, PUBLISH_DATE)>
<!ELEMENT REVIEWED #PCDATA>
<!ATTLIST REVIEWED
     ID                      NMTOKEN                   #REQUIRED
>
<!ELEMENT HEADLINE #PCDATA>
<!ELEMENT ABSTRACT #PCDATA>
<!ELEMENT CREATE_DATE #CDATA>
<!ATTLIST CREATE_DATE
     DATE                    CDATA                     #REQUIRED
>
<!ELEMENT LASTMOD_DATE #CDATA>
<!ATTLIST LASTMOD_DATE
     DATE                    CDATA                     #REQUIRED
>
<!ELEMENT PUBLISH_DATE #CDATA>
<!ATTLIST PUBLISH_DATE
     DATE                    CDATA                     #REQUIRED
>
```

In this example, you'll note that the content models for some of our elements are defined as PCDATA. This stands for "Parseable Character Data," as opposed to character data (CDATA), which we saw in our first example in the section Building a DTD. PCDATA content can include parseable items such as other tags. Any "mixed content" areas of your document, where you want to combine text and tags, have a content model of PCDATA.

The Body

The body of the XML instance is where all the really interesting stuff happens. The head has a tightly constrained content model, whereas the body is full of mixed content, that is, parseable character data mixed with elements. In the body of the document, you first realize why using XML is a great way to represent this kind of data. XML brings structure to the unstructured world of narrativelike data.

Let's examine what we want to do in the document body. The body should include the following:

1. Normal text markup features, such as bold, italic, and underline.
2. Headings to delineate one section of a review from another.
3. Actor names, movie names, and director names must be links into a search facility of some kind.
4. Links to other reviews.
5. Links to outside URLs.

The first item designates normal markup features. For simplicity's sake we're going to borrow HTML-style markup for things like italics, bold, and headings; there's no need to reinvent the wheel.

Item 3 is actually "two, two, two items in one!" In Chapter 4, we figured out that directors and actors are both "people" (remember the person entity in Chapter 4?). Looking back at the data model diagram (in Figure 4-5), we see we're also tracking movies as entities. Thus we need some way to mark a word or phrase within the text of our review as having to do with a movie or a person. Items 4 and 5 both fit into the same category, linking a part of the instance to some external entity. Let's take a closer look at linking.

Linking Up: XLink

If you're familiar with HTML and the Web, you think of a link as an underlined phrase or image that, when clicked, triggers a Web browser to fetch another page. This relatively familiar paradigm is only one kind of link: a *hypertext link*. XML and XLink, the recently completed XML Linking Language specification, enable you to define many more link properties and behaviors. Any XML tag can be defined as having the properties of a link.

XML Linking Language (XLink)

The XLink specification is a redefinition of linking. If you're a Web user, you probably think of a link as "something you click to go somewhere else." The concept of a "link" is key to the metaphor of the Web. Once you *get* the way links work, the user interface of the Web suddenly makes sense. It's an immensely valuable idea, but the XLink spec rigorously attempts to define and enlarge this idea. With XLink linking, links can be bidirectional, they can be managed so that they never go "stale," and they enable you to add your own links from documents you don't own.

One immediate benefit of XLink is a syntax that enables you to represent links generically in your XLink documents in a way that can be reflected easily in a link database (because each link is assigned a unique ID). For that reason and because it's a good idea to support standards (remember the Rosetta stone), it's a good idea to use the XLink syntax, but don't get too bogged down in the details.

For a full description of the XLink spec syntax, check out http://www.w3.org/TR/xlink/. Tim Bray has also written a primer on XLink at http://www.xml.com/pub/a/2000/09/xlink/.

The following DTD fragment is an example of how to implement the movie element using the XLink syntax. XLink requires the definition of the following attributes: type (the kind of link it is), href (what it's linking to, the hypertext reference), show (what should happen when the link is actuated, either clicked or the equivalent action in whatever interface you're dealing with), and actuate (how the link is actuated, either by user action or by default on the page loading). It's beyond the scope of this book to go into all the permutations of these options. Suffice it to say that the kinds of links we're talking about are locator links (they locate another resource, such as a page, URL, movie title, and so on). Clicking on them *replaces* what the user is looking at. The user must click the link to activate it, so activate's value is onRequest.

```
<!ELEMENT movie ANY>
<!ATTLIST movie
```

XML Design

```
        xlink:type          (simple|extended|locator|arc)
                                              #FIXED "locator"
        <!-- This is a locator link because it points to an external
             resource -->
        xlink:href          CDATA                   #REQUIRED
        xlink:show          (new | embed | replace)    "replace"
        <!-- When link is actuated (such as with a click) should the linked-to
             data come up in a new window, be embedded in the current window or
             replace the current content? -->
        xlink:actuate       (onRequest |onLoad)        "onRequest"
        <!-- How should the link be activated? Default is on user request
             (for example, the user clicks on the link text) -->
>
```

This DTD fragment instantiates our movie element as a simple link using the XLink syntax. Those familiar with HTML may find it strange to use the href keyword where it isn't pointing to a URL. In XLink language, an href is just a way to point to an external resource. In this case, we're pointing to a movie, a record of which is stored in a relational database table (and therefore is referenced by a numerical ID).

The preceding example might look complex, but because most of the attributes are implied or fixed, they aren't required in the actual code. A sample of our new movie element looks like this:

```
<MOVIE xlink:href="12345">Ben Hur</MOVIE>
```

That's it! If we assume that our PERSON and REVIEW elements are going to be similarly defined, we come up with the following full XML instance for both our MOVIE and PERSON elements:

```
<?xml version="1.0">
<CYBERCINEMA_REVIEW ID="123">
    <HEAD>
        <!-- Header information goes here -->
        <AUTHOR_BLOCK>
```

```
                <AUTHOR ID="2">Daniel Appelquist</AUTHOR>
            </AUTHOR_BLOCK>
            <REVIEWED ID="12345">Spartacus</REVIEWED>
            <HEADLINE>Roman Holiday</HEADLINE>
            <ABSTRACT>This film marks the pinnacle of historical action
            drama.</ABSTRACT>
            <CREATE_DATE DATE="2000-05-17T17:10:00,0"/>
            <LASTMOD_DATE DATE="2000-05-17T18:12:00,0"/>
            <PUBLISH_DATE DATE="2000-05-17T19:27:00,0"/>
        </HEAD>
        <BODY>
            <!-- Body information goes here  -->
            The film <MOVIE link:href="12345">Spartacus</MOVIE> stars <PERSON
            link:href ="932">Tony Curtis</PERSON> as a fun-loving slave. Often
            confused with
            <MOVIE link:href="12346">Ben Hur</MOVIE> (see our <REVIEW
            link:href ="876">review</REVIEW>), this 1960's classic is...
        </BODY>
</CYBERCINEMA_REVIEW>
```

It gets really interesting when you store these links in your relational database, which I describe in Chapter 6.

After you've properly identified the movie titles and the names of people in the body of the review, it's up to you how you want those elements to appear in the representation of this review to the viewing public. (See the Appendix for the complete CyberCinema DTD.)

One challenge when dealing with links (XLinks and otherwise) is keeping them fresh. Using XLink enables you to keep links fresh, but your application still has to do some work.

Keeping References Current

References to other movies should enable end users to locate reviews of those movies, even if the reviews are written and/or published later. You don't want to modify every review that references *Spartacus* just because someone wrote a new review of it. Your application should keep these references current for you. As you add reviews, you link them to movies through their database IDs. In most cases, you shouldn't have to change already created XML just because you're adding something new.

Deleting items (such as reviews) is another matter, and it is more complicated. If you delete a review, for instance, and five other reviews are linked to this review, you'll have to remove the links in those five reviews before the database will actually enable you to remove the review you're trying to remove (thanks to relational integrity). Although you can do this, it's not very efficient. Hence, *be careful* about which pieces of data you "decompose," that is, extract from the XML and store in the relational database.

You may want to consider adding an "inactive" flag to your database table where your content is stored. That way, you can delete items by turning this flag on, and you won't have to worry about traversing many documents if you want to delete one of them. In fact, I never delete anything; I simply flag certain items as inactive, enabling me to recover them later if I've made a mistake. It also enables me to retain relational integrity in my database without having to jump through hoops. I'll discuss this further in Chapter 6 when we get into relational schema design.

Dealing with Arbitrary Binary Data

Another thorny issue when dealing with content in the bodies of your XML instances is what to do with binary data. Especially in the framework of content management, you often find yourself dealing with nontext data, such as images, sounds, video, and smells.[1] There are two approaches to mixing XML and binary data:

- Point to the binary data externally (as in an external file on the file system or in a database or as in a Uniform Resource Identifier—URI—that points to the data). This is the approach that HTML has

---

[1] Don't laugh; a company called DigiScents (www.digiscents.com) is doing just this. Very cool stuff.

taken. The big problem here is data synchronization. For example (taken from XHTML):

```
<image src="http://www.torgo.com/torgo.gif"/>
```

- Encode the binary data in the XML document itself, using base64 encoding. The problem here is that encoding binary data whenever you want to store it and decoding it again when you want to use it isn't terribly efficient. For example:

```
<image dt:dt="binary.base64">84592gv8Z53815b82bA68g</image>
```

The preceding *encodes* the binary data into a string of numbers and letters, using the base64 encoding algorithm, a commonly used encoding standard, encoders, and decoders that are built in to many programming environments (Java and Perl, to name two).

Deciding which is the best approach depends on your application. If you're managing content in an internal application (that is, you're not packaging content to send to other businesses), you shouldn't go through the bother of encoding binary data into the XML documents. It's better to use an external reference. However, if you're shipping your XML over the Internet or over a private network to customers and other businesses, it makes sense to "wrap up" the binary data with the XML when you send it (as with the base64 encoding example).

Extensible Hypertext Markup Language

XHTML stands for eXtensible HyperText Markup Language, but it's more descriptive to call it "XML-compliant HTML." It's HTML that has been slightly modified to make it comply with XML. For instance, (if you're familiar with HTML), the HTML tag for image is `<IMAGE SRC="foo.gif">`. That's an illegal construct in XML because in XML every open tag has to be accompanied by a close tag in order to preserve the tree-structure of the data in an XML document. Equivalent XHTML for this would be

```
<IMAGE SRC="foo.gif"></IMAGE>
```

or simply

```
<IMAGE SRC="foo.gif"/>
```

The latter is shorthand for the former.

Likewise, the `<BR>` tag (another tag that appears alone) must be represented as `<BR/>`. The rest of XHTML is similarly defined. Another important difference between HTML and XHTML is the use of the `<P>` tag. In HTML, the `<P>` tag is often used just to insert some white space. In XHTML, the `<P>` tag is an enclosing tag:

```
<P>This is a paragraph</P>
```

All tags are containers; this conceptual difference is one of the most difficult concepts for HTML jockeys to understand about XHTML. Actually, having `<P>` tag without a corresponding end tag has been technically illegal since HTML 2.0, but because no Web browsers enforced this rule, this has been the de facto usage. Because XHTML (and all documents written in XML-derived languages) must be well formed, that kind of sloppiness is no longer allowed.

Building XML DTDs: Let the Experts Do the Hard Stuff

In providing examples of DTDs earlier in this chapter, I found it handy to pick and choose DTD fragments from elsewhere (such as from HTML or from DTD samples available in public Internet repositories) and then combine them to suit my needs. However, be warned: You should first understand how DTDs are constructed and how to define them properly. Only then should you use this technique as a means of minimizing the time it takes to define a DTD for your needs. Luckily, an entire community of XML professionals is more than willing to put their work in the public domain. The best way to become a competent DTD author is to read the DTDs (and DTD documentation) that others have produced.

I have limited the number of URLs provided in this book because they often go stale (especially when they're provided in printed documents), so the ones in this section are the URLs to the home pages for these sites. You can use these URLs as starting points in your search for XML resources and information. In particular, these sites provide DTD examples and fragments and DTDs tailored for specific needs.

- **W3C at http://www.w3.org.** Go to the source: the World Wide Web Consortium maintains an archive of XML DTDs and specifications and provides supporting documentation. This is an excellent resource for anyone building DTDs and should be your first stop.
- **XML Catalog at http://www.xml.org.** This is probably the best overall site for pointers to XML resources on the Web. The XML Catalog area is a particularly good place to look for industry-specific DTDs and DTD fragments. Financial reporting? Check out the Accounting section. Building documents about the next generation space shuttle? Check out the Space section. You never knew so many disciplines were using XML of one kind or another.
- **Resources at http://www.xml.com.** As the name suggests, xml.com is more commercially oriented than xml.org, which can be both a good and a bad thing. You'll see more links to interesting projects being worked on in the commercial software community, but less funky leading edge stuff. Both xml.org and xml.com are good places to look, and no DTD scavenging session is complete without them.
- **xCBL (XML Common Business Library) at http://www.xcbl.org.** xCBL is an excellent resource for business-oriented XML DTD fragments and other resources.

Summary

XML design is a creative process and requires intuitive thinking. In this chapter, I've shown you an approach to XML design that I've used with some success. The value of XML is that you don't need to be a professional information designer to start using it in projects. And once you start using it, you begin thinking of new uses for it, new places where it can fit to enhance reliability and interoperability.

If there's an XML DTD that already does what you need it to do, use it; it will save you some of the trouble and headache of building your own DTD. If you're lucky, you may find a DTD that is close to your needs. This DTD may even have been designed by a consortium or industry group that you can join, which enables you to participate in its further development. Joining industry groups like these can pay off in other ways, as well; you are exposed to the ideas and thinking of other industry professionals.

If you're looking for a more comprehensive reference to XML design and application, you can't go wrong with *Just XML* by John E. Simpson (2000). For the full DTD for our CyberCinema example, see the Appendix.

So, where does the SQL bit come in? In the next chapter, we'll discuss SQL schema design and integration of the schema with XML.

Chapter 6

Getting Relational: Database Schema Design

> In which my car leaves me stranded on the highway, and we finally discuss the integration of XML and SQL!

A database schema is a collection of database objects that are designed together to fulfill a specific function. The most commonly known database object is a database table, in which information is stored in columns and rows (see the section Structured Query Language (SQL) in Chapter 2), but other commonly used database objects include sequences (incremental number generators), stored procedures (sometimes called by database-specific terms such as Oracle's PL/SQL), and triggers (stored procedures that "fire off" before, during, or after a specific event, like the insertion or deletion of data).

In this chapter, we discuss how to put together a database schema that best complements the storage of data in XML form. We start with database schema basics and then delve into more detailed examples. The underlying principle presented in this chapter is that of *partial decomposition*, a method for integrating XML with relational databases by which the entire XML instance is stored *as a whole* (possibly in the database itself), and *selected* data from the XML instances is extracted and placed in relational tables to speed access to data and to maintain data integrity.

Knowing When to Let Go

When I was commuting back and forth to Baltimore from Washington D.C., having a car was absolutely essential. Every morning I drove an hour up, and every evening I drove an hour back. One morning in the middle of highway traffic on the way to Baltimore, my otherwise wonderful used Saab 900 completely died. Without warning, the engine quit on me. I was barely able to veer across three lanes of traffic into the breakdown lane before the car sputtered to a stop. The Saab, which had been great for moving me around, simply wasn't up to the rigors of a daily drive, of more than 100 miles. The long and short of it is that I got the Saab fixed, but because I wanted to make sure a breakdown didn't happen to me again, I bought a new car (actually new).

What's my point here? After building an abstract data model and writing a still fairly abstract DTD (see Chapter 5, XML Design), it's time to get a little less abstract. If XML is in the driver's seat, the relational database and the database schema you instantiate inside it are the tires, suspension, exhaust system, and engine—the vehicle itself. Remember, a car, no matter how much you love it, is replaceable. You might love driving your two-door roadster around when you're 22 and single, but it may be somewhat impractical for dropping Billy and Sue off at soccer practice. Likewise, your relational database and database schema are a vehicle—a way to get your data from point a to point b; they are application specific. Your database and database schema eventually will be scrapped and replaced with something better. Your XML data, on the other hand, will live on.

The important point is not to get bogged down in the database schema design. Do it right, but don't fall into the trap of thinking your database schema has to support everything in your data model. Your SQL schema should first and foremost support the functionality you need in your application *now*. If you can make small additions to your schema that will make it easier to support functions you think you will *probably* need in the near future, by all means make them, but don't go overboard.

First Steps

A database schema revolves around tables, so the first step in creating a schema is to determine the tables that are needed and then determine how they relate to each other. To do this, you work forward from the requirements, data modeling, and DTD design work you've already completed. Let's return to our simple e-mail application. As in all stages of application development, we must review the requirements (we wrote these in Chapter 3; refer to that chapter if you need to review the process of gathering requirements):

- A user must be able to write an e-mail message.
- A user must be able to send e-mail to another user.
- A user must be able to read e-mail sent to him from another user.
- An e-mail will consist of a subject line and a message body.

And because we have a data model diagram (from Chapter 4), let's review that as well (see Figure 6-1).

Finally, we have to consider the DTD we built in Chapter 5. Refer to Appendix A for the complete CyberCinema DTD.

Looking at our data model diagram in Figure 6-1, we're going to need, at the bare minimum, a user table and an e-mail message table, a table for each of the data entities represented in the diagram. Because the DTD we built in

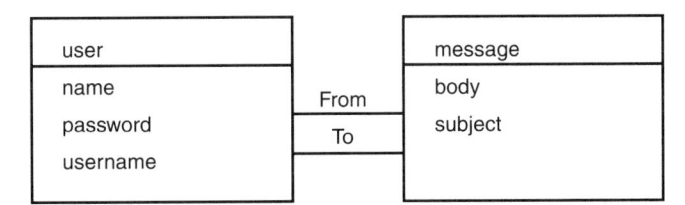

Figure 6-1: Data modeling diagram for e-mail system

Chapter 5 is built around the e-mail messages themselves, the XML instances (the e-mail messages themselves) are stored in the e-mail messages table.

XML Storage

I tend to store things like XML and images in the database itself. Another approach is to store so-called "large objects" like these on the file system and reference them from the database; that is, instead of including the actual XML in the database, include a path name to the location of the XML file in the file system.

I don't recommend this second approach to XML storage for a number of reasons:

1. It isn't as scalable as providing the XML in the database. In order to access an XML file when using the file system reference solution, you first have to make a database call and then actually go to the file system to get the file. This operation can be quite expensive to perform, and you haven't even started parsing your XML file yet.

2. The file system reference solution doesn't lend itself well to replication. Creating a "replicant" database (for disaster recovery purposes, for instance) is more difficult.

3. You can't write XML logic into the database. It's sometimes desirable to add to the database an XML processing layer (for instance, a trigger that performs XML decomposition, which we discuss in the section Enter Partial Decomposition later in this chapter). When your XML is outside the database, writing an XML processing layer isn't an option or is more difficult and/or less scalable.

4. Backups are more reliable when the XML is part of the database. It makes your backup strategy simpler and more foolproof, if all your data is in the same place, instead of having some data located in one place (the database) and the rest located somewhere else (the file system). Storing XML in the database means your backups are more likely to work, and when you have to recover your database from backups, one less procedure is required.

The database schema designs presented in this book assume large object storage in the database. If, for whatever misguided reason, you decide to put your large objects on the file system, the principles I'm going to present are still quite valid. Just don't come crying to me.

So what does the database schema look like? As mentioned previously, we need a table for our e-mail messages and a table for our users. Both tables will contain a numerical ID as their primary key field. That leaves us with the following database schema, represented here by SQL CREATE TABLE statements (the statements you would use as the database administrator to create the tables):

```
CREATE TABLE message (
        message_id       INTEGER(16)      NOT NULL,
        message_xml      CLOB             NOT NULL,
);
CREATE TABLE user (
        user_id          INTEGER(16)      NOT NULL,
        user_name        VARCHAR(64)      NOT NULL
);
```

SQL Examples

I'm using "pseudo-SQL" for the printed examples throughout this book. You can't expect to type in these statements and see actual tables materialize in your database. "Standard" SQL (which I sometimes pronounce "squeal" as in "squeal like a pig") varies considerably depending on what database product you're using. I've used Sybase and Oracle and SQL Server, and I have a smattering of experience with Informix and MySql. The same principles should apply to all these systems. Database schema definition files for Oracle are provided on the CD that accompanies this book.

For all examples in which I'm storing XML in the database, I'm using the CLOB datatype. CLOB stands for Character Large OBject (nobody ever said software engineers could spell) and is one of SQL1999's new datatypes. If your database doesn't support CLOBs, you could use any character-oriented datatype your database does support. For instance, some databases have a TEXT datatype that serves this purpose. Note that use of these datatypes (as compared to CHAR or VARCHAR) often means you take a performance hit. The advantage of using CLOB datatypes is that you aren't limited to a certain size (although there is usually an upper bound on CLOB size—approximately 1MB).

I'm also using unique numerical ID numbers quite a lot (as in the e-mail example, with `message_id`). The underlying assumption is that something is creating these unique IDs. This capacity is built in to some databases; others require that you write a trigger to assign the ID when a new row is inserted. Either way, the ID usually comes from a sequence produced within the database, thereby guaranteeing uniqueness.

Great! We're done!

Wait a second, hold the phone! We're not leveraging the power of our RDBMS. What fools these mortals be! What we have from the previous example is great as long as the database doesn't have to be able to answer the request "list the e-mail messages I've received"—an essential request in any e-mail system. Databases are smart, but they can't tell you what they don't know. If you want your relational database to answer requests like this—to "know" about your data instead of simply storing it—you need to tell it about your data in the first place. In XML terminology, you need to *decompose* the XML into your relational tables.

SQL and XML: The Joys of Partial Decomposition

XML is great at structuring data. Relational databases are great at storing and relating data. How do you get the best out of these two different ways of looking at data? You can create a table that contains a row for each part of your XML document. For example, take the following XML fragment:

```
The <b>quick</b> brown <i>fox</i> jumped over the <u>lazy</u> dog.
```

Some database packages implement a "persistent parse tree" database schema to store XML. What this means is that the entire XML document is decomposed, element by element, into individual nodes (see Figure 2-2 from Chapter 2), and each node is stored as a separate row in a database table, a table not specific to any particular XML language but able to accept any XML data. With this scheme, you need up to 13 rows of a table just to represent the preceding line of XML code. Each node of the tree is put in its own row, with relations built to the other nodes to reflect the original structure and order of the XML. The original XML document is essentially disintegrated, broken into its constituent parts and stored atomically. Yes, you could answer the question "Which words in all of my documents are bold?" But in order to do so, your database has to select across all these rows. In addition, such database schemas don't lend themselves well to indexing. And what about relational integrity? In the following fragment, how do you relate the reference to Charade back to a relational table of movie titles kept elsewhere in your database?

```
<movie id="3234">Charade</movie> is one of Cary Grant's later and least well known films.
```

Another method for integrating XML with a SQL database is *XML decomposition*. An XML decomposition database schema takes the opposite approach to persistent parse trees by creating a schema that entirely encompasses your XML documents. Every element, as well as every single attribute of each element, has a separate table. Rigid relational integrity is maintained, but at the price of flexibility. Also, unstructured data (such as a flow of text with tags embedded at various points—like our CyberCinema reviews) is very difficult to support. With full decomposition, you throw away the XML when you decompose it into the SQL database because you don't need it any more. You've fully encoded your information in the database, and you should be able to recreate your XML instance if needed from that stored information. However, XML schema evolution (such as adding to your DTD) means SQL schema evolution, which can then lead to changing application code. Therefore decomposition is useful only when you have a rigidly defined XML schema that you know will never change, which is never.

Both persistent parse trees and decomposition are misguided attempts to integrate XML and SQL tightly.

Enter Partial Decomposition

In contrast to the methods for XML/SQL integration described previously, partial decomposition is a simple method that can help manage some of the complexity inherent in a mixed XML/SQL-based system. The components of partial decomposition are the following:

- Store the entire XML instance in the database.
- Keep the XML instance as the primary source of data.
- Extract *selected* data from the XML, and place it in relational tables for quick access and relational constraint management.

Partial decomposition really struts its stuff in the application of these rules. With partial decomposition, we take a different approach: Let XML do what it's good at (structuring content), and let SQL do what it's good at (enforcing relational constraints and organizing data).

Partial decomposition is a loose integration of XML and SQL. You can still use persistent parse trees with partial decomposition. In fact, it doesn't matter how you store the XML itself. The key to partial decomposition is figuring out what this *selected* data that you want to store in the database is. The *selected* data depends on the purpose of the application and the data.

Let's go back to two strengths of SQL databases.

Enforcing Relational Constraints

With e-mail messages, you want your database to ensure that the To and From fields refer to real users. Relational databases can do this for you if you design your partial decomposition schema to include a user table and constraints that the To and From fields must refer to rows in this user table. Hence, we need To and From fields (that is, columns) in our e-mail table.

Organizing Data for Easy Recall

Organizing data really means answering questions about your data. The question you need to ask yourself is "What questions is my application going to ask the database?" In this case, we want to be able to answer the request: "List the e-mail messages a particular user has received." The To and From columns already solve this problem for e-mail messages.

We end up with the following schema, represented by SQL create statements:

```
CREATE TABLE message (
        message_id      INTEGER(16)     NOT NULL          PRIMARY KEY,
        message_xml     CLOB            NOT NULL,
        message_from    INTEGER(16)     REFERENCES user(user_id)     NOT NULL,
        message_to      INTEGER(16)     REFERENCES user(user_id)     NOT NULL,
);
```

```
CREATE TABLE user (
      user_id          INTEGER(16)    NOT NULL       PRIMARY KEY,
      user_name        VARCHAR(64)    NOT NULL
);
```

First, for our e-mail messages we're building a simple table that has a unique numerical key (which is important) and stores the whole of each XML instance in a CLOB field. The other two columns in the e-mail message table, To and From, are numerical and refer to rows in the other table we're creating—a user table.

CLOBs Part Two

In using CLOBs, it is often desirable (depending on your database server) to isolate the CLOBs into their own table for performance reasons. Applying this to the previous example, we get:

```
CREATE TABLE message_content {
    message_id     INTEGER(16)    REFERENCES message(message_id) NOT NULL,
    message_xml    CLOB           NOT NULL
}

CREATE TABLE message {
    message_id     INTEGER(16)    PRIMARY KEY NOT NULL,
    message_from   INTEGER(16)    REFERENCES user(user_id) NOT NULL,
    message_to     INTEGER(16)    REFERENCES user(user_id) NOT NULL
}
```

In this case, we've stored everything *about* the message in the message table itself, but we put the content of the message to the side in a message_content table. This approach is sometimes faster; the DB engine can cache more of the message_info table because it doesn't have to store the CLOBs in memory with the other data. Hence, queries against the message_info table are faster than queries against your combined table. In practice, a well-tuned application would not even load the XML into memory until required. The efficacy of all this depends on your database vendor and the application logic that you're connecting to it. A skilled database administrator can help you determine which approach will make the most sense for your data and your application.

The mechanism of partial decomposition now kicks in: Whenever you insert a new e-mail message into the message table or update a message already there, you have to examine the XML instance, decompose the information you're interested in, and insert or update the corresponding rows in your relational schema. This can happen in your application code as part of a transaction or (in databases that allow for complex coding within the database itself) as a trigger on the table. If you violate an integrity constraint (for example, your e-mail message XML instance contains a From field with a user ID that doesn't correspond to a user in the relational user table), you roll back the whole transaction and kick back an error. Relational integrity is maintained. If you want a list of a user's e-mail messages, a simple SQL query is all that is required:

```
select * from message where message_to = 3
```

To read the actual message, you pull out the XML and transform it as necessary for the display medium you're using.

Using Partial Decomposition as a Caching Strategy

Another way to use the tool of partial decomposition is to extract bits of data you want close at hand in your relational table. For instance, it is preferable to get the subject line of each message from the database, instead of having to retrieve each XML instance (that is, the e-mail message), parse it, and pull out each subject every time you have to display a list of messages.

Add the message subject line to our relational schema, like so:

```
CREATE TABLE message (
        message_id        INTEGER(16)     NOT NULL        PRIMARY KEY,
        message_xml       CLOB            NOT NULL,
        message_subject   VARCHAR(255)    NOT NULL,
        message_from      INTEGER(16)     REFERENCES user(user_id)    NOT NULL,
        message_to        INTEGER(16)     REFERENCES user(user_id)    NOT NULL,
);
```

In addition, adding subject line decomposition to our partial decomposition, we can do just that.

Data Synchronization with Partial Decomposition

Whenever you have data mirrored in two places at once, the data could become corrupt, that is, the data in your relational table might not match the data in your XML file. This can happen for any number of reasons; for instance, the routines you're using for partial decomposition could fail halfway through, leaving your data only partially decomposed. Following are some strategies for keeping your data in sync:

- **Remember to keep XML in the driver's seat.** Don't be tempted to update the rows of your table directly from your application code. Let your partial decomposition routines continue to do this based on your XML. By compartmentalizing the population of these tables in one segment of your code, the decomposition, you ensure that the data in the tables is always a mirror of the data in the XML itself. The system is also easier to maintain; when you want to add something to your decomposition, all the code is in one place (either as a part of your application code or in the database itself).

- **Use database transactions.** If your code first inserts or updates an XML instance in your database and then inserts or updates rows associated with this XML instance, make this part of one database *transaction*. You can start a transaction, do all the inserts and updates you want, and then end the transaction, committing all changes at once. That way, if anything goes wrong halfway through, the database automatically rolls back all your changes and kicks back an exception, which you can catch and do something intelligent with (such as writing an error log that can alert support staff of a potential problem before your users start complaining about it).

- **Build data management utilities.** You should have a way to rebuild all the partial decomposition information from your XML, and you should do this on a regular basis (depending on how much data you have). Rebuilding the partial decomposition information from your XML continually maintains consistent data and alerts you to potential problems before they balloon into big cleanup jobs. Your rebuild should be resilient enough to flag errors and then move on so that you can run it overnight and fix problems in the morning. You also should build small utilities for bulk deletes and bulk updates.

In general, think of the data stored in the partial decomposition tables as an index, not as the actual data. The data really is stored in only one place: the XML.

Problems with Partial Decomposition

Partial decomposition is especially geared toward write-sometimes-read-mostly applications. Whenever you make changes to your data, the data has to go through the partial decomposition step, which (depending on the complexity of your data) can be costly in terms of performance. If you made only one change, it's also wasteful because all the characteristics from your XML instance are decomposed each time you change it. Document management systems, such as the one we're describing in the CyberCinema example, are particularly suited to this approach because once a document is published, it basically sits there and is read repeatedly.

Another problem with partial decomposition is with schema evolution (using the word "schema" in a general sense—anything relating to changing your data model). If your data must be changed and, therefore, your DTD must change, your schema for partial decomposition may also have to change. The good news is that it doesn't *always* have to change, only when you want to decompose new elements. And even then, it's an additive process.

It's important to keep these issues in mind when you're analyzing the performance characteristics of your application. Of course, the subject of application performance is a more complex issue, and entire books are dedicated to the subject of performance analysis and writing "performant" code (like "performant" is a real word—they're not fooling anyone).

Decomposing CyberCinema

Let's turn to our more complex example of the CyberCinema Web site. Let's revisit our skeletal requirements:

- Reviewers must be able to write reviews.
- Reviews must be searchable by movie.
- Reviews must be searchable by director.
- Reviews must be searchable by actor.
- Reviews must be searchable by reviewer.
- Movies must be searchable by director.
- Movies must be searchable by actor.

Now refer to the XML DTD for CyberCinema that we built in Chapter 5 (see Appendix A).

Finally, we'll bring to bear our data model diagram (see Figure 6-2).

First, we determine the tables required for our database. From reviewing our data model in Figure 6-2, we find the minimal tables we need are a table for movie reviews (which will be the table containing our XML review instances), a table for movies, and a table for people (such as reviewers, actors, and directors). Because people can have different roles (that is, reviewers, actors, and directors) within our system, it makes sense to create a table for people and a separate table for roles people can play. That way, if we want to add a role (such as producer or screenwriter) and start tracking people in that role in addition to the three roles we've already identified, we don't have to go through SQL schema evolution.

From reviewing our requirements, we've got a list of requests with which we want to be able to query the database:

- List the review of a given movie.
- List the reviews by a given reviewer.
- List the movies in which a given actor acted.
- List the movies that a given director directed.
- List the reviews that relate to a given actor.
- List the reviews that relate to a given director.

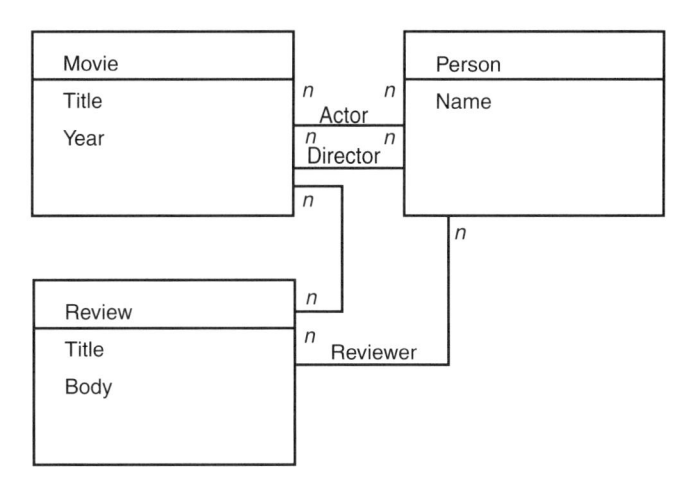

Figure 6-2: CyberCinema data model diagram

Let's take a look at our person and role tables first because they're the simplest:

```
CREATE TABLE person (
    person_id       INTEGER(16)     NOT NULL    PRIMARY KEY,
    person_name     VARCHAR(255)    NOT NULL
);
CREATE TABLE role (
    role_id         INTEGER(16)     NOT NULL    PRIMARY KEY,
    role_name       VARCHAR(255)    NOT NULL
);
CREATE TABLE person_role (
    person_id   INTEGER(16) NOT NULL REFERENCES person(person_id),
    role_id     INTEGER(16) NOT NULL REFERENCES role(role_id)
    PRIMARY KEY (person_id, role_id)
);
```

Notice that, in addition to creating a person and a role table, we've also created a bridging table, person_role. Now people in our database can have more than one role. We've already solved the "Woody Allen" bug.[1] We've also solved the "Roger Ebert" bug[2] (people can be movie reviewers *and* be actors). Also, by making the combination of the columns unique as the primary key, we've forced uniqueness on person_id and role_id so that a given person can't be in the table with the same role more than once (which wouldn't make sense). Already, our system is surging with power, and we haven't even injected our XML into the mixture!

Bridging Tables

"Bridging tables" is my name for tables that exist solely to bridge the gap between two different tables. They're sometimes called linking tables, but we're throwing

---

[1.] Woody Allen writes, directs, and stars in most of his own films.
[2.] Roger Ebert, famous for being a movie reviewer, has also appeared in some films (usually playing himself).

around the word "link" in some other contexts here, so I'm sticking to "bridge." Any time you want to create a relationship between two different tables, you should use a bridging table. You can simply include a reference in one table directly to the other table (as we saw in the book database example in Chapter 2), but doing so is actually bad practice for anything other than the simplest uses of SQL databases. Using bridging tables provides much more flexibility. In the book database example, for instance, we couldn't have stored any books with multiple authors the way I did it (with a direct reference from one table to another). With the addition of a bridging table that contains references to both the books table and the authors table, multiple authors per book are possible.

Now let's take a look at movies:

```
CREATE TABLE movie (
    movie_id        INTEGER(16)     NOT NULL    PRIMARY KEY,
    movie_name      VARCHAR(255)    NOT NULL,
    movie_date      DATE            NOT NULL
);
```

Name and date are probably all we need to identify a movie uniquely. You rarely see two movies come out with the same title in the same year—it tends to confuse the viewing public.

Dates

The reason I've chosen to use a SQL DATE data type for the previous example is that the database now can respond reliably to requests like "list the movies that were released between 1987 and 1989" by interrogating the database. Even though this request isn't one of the ones we're presently making, it doesn't hurt to think ahead. The database can also return the date information to you in whatever format you need it. Don't be afraid to take advantage of the features of your RDBMS.

For our system to be able to respond to the last two requests (listing reviews that relate to given actors and listing reviews that relate to given directors), we also have to build bridging tables to bridge people and movies. But wait a second—what are these bridging tables really bridging? Movies to people? Actually, they're bridging movies to people's roles. At least, they are if you want to be able to respond to the request "list the movies a given person acts in."

So our movies to people's roles table looks like this:

```
CREATE TABLE movie_person_role (
    movie_id    INTEGER(16) NOT NULL REFERENCES movie(movie_id),
    person_id   INTEGER(16) NOT NULL REFERENCES person(person_id),
    role_id     INTEGER(16) NOT NULL REFERENCES role(role_id),
    PRIMARY KEY (person_id, role_id, movie_id)
);
```

Now we've got an interconnecting web of movies and people that, after it's populated with data, can give us instant filmographies on any given person and tell us who directed or acted in any given movie. SQL rocks!

XML Nitro Injection: Adding Reviews

Now we're ready to add our review table. As we did earlier, let's start with a database schema that uses partial decomposition for maintaining data integrity. First we need a table to hold our reviews:

```
CREATE TABLE review (
    review_id   INTEGER(16)   NOT NULL    PRIMARY KEY,
    review_xml  CLOB          NOT NULL
);
```

Let's add the following bridging tables:

```
CREATE TABLE review_movie (
    review_id   INTEGER(16)   NOT NULL    REFERENCES review(review_id),
    movie_id    INTEGER(16)   NOT NULL    REFERENCES movie(movie_id),
    PRIMARY KEY (review_id, movie_id)
```

```
);
CREATE TABLE review_person (
    review_id    INTEGER(16)    NOT NULL    REFERENCES review(review_id),
    person_id    INTEGER(16)    NOT NULL    REFERENCES person(person_id),
    PRIMARY KEY (review_id, person_id)
);
```

Notice that we're not bridging to the `person_role` table for reviews as we do for movies. That's because the XML itself (as described in Chapter 5) doesn't include a role attribute for the person element, and it doesn't really need to. During decomposition, we won't know from the XML instance which role this particular person played in the film being reviewed, but we don't really need to know.

During XML decomposition, when you see the following:

```
<review id="123"> … <person id="2345">Pauly Shore</person>'s movies are
largely misunderstood works of genius. … </review>
```

your insert into the database looks something like this:

```
INSERT INTO review_person (review_id, person_id)  VALUES(123, 2345);
```

And because the XML decomposition happens when the XML is inserted into the database, you end up building an accurate relational map of everything you've chosen to decompose.

Link Management

Managing the links between documents (especially large numbers of documents) can be an arduous task. For example, so-called "link rot" on the Web often turns Web surfing into a frustrating experience. You click on one link and then another, only to find that the links lead to dead ends: error (404) screens, error messages from your browser, and the like. This phenomenon is due to a lack of link management. When Webmasters decide to remove a page from a Web site, they have no reliable way to find out how many pages link to it, so they have no way to determine the extent of the link rot they're causing. Similarly, people hosting lists of links have no way of knowing that a particular page they're linked to has been removed. At best, they can go through their list of links on a regular basis and try to sweep out the rubbish, but it's a losing battle.

Rewriting URLs

The problem of bad links is pervasive, and instituting good link management at the content management layer is one solution. However, skillful Webmasters have other tools that they can use to combat this problem. One way is to rewrite URLs on the fly within the Web server. This technique can be especially useful when you're making major changes to your Web infrastructure (such as moving from one publishing system to another). Apache's mod_rewrite (if you're using Apache as a Web server, which I highly recommend) is the pinnacle of achievement in this area. It enables you automatically to rewrite URLs on a request-by-request basis, using rules that can be as complex as you want them to be.

For instance, say your URLs are all in the form http://www.torgo.com/news/1234.html, where "1234" is an article or object ID number. Because of a change in your site's architecture (for example, instituting an XML-based publishing system), you want to change all your URLs to be in the form http://www.torgo.com/articles.jhtml?article_id=1234. If you institute a mod_rewrite rule to transform the string "news/<number>.html" into "articles.jhtml?article_id=<number>", then you've proofed your site against everyone who bookmarked older articles or otherwise linked to your articles from other sites you may not know of. That's only the bare minimum that the wonders of mod_rewrite can achieve.

At this writing, the URL for mod_rewrite is http://httpd.apache.org/docs/mod/mod_rewrite.html.

The problem of link rot on the Web is pervasive and nasty, and there's no ready solution for it. While it's annoying to get a 404 message in response to clicking a link, I can be forgiving in most cases. I'm astounded when I get an error clicking on a link to a page within the *same site*. That kind of nonsense is completely preventable, as you'll see.

In Chapter 5, we added a link syntax (XLink) to link reviews to movies, people, and other reviews (see the section Linking Up: XLink in Chapter 5). With all of these links, but especially in linking reviews to other reviews, the concept of link management is key.

Reviewing the DTD syntax we have for our links, we see that the sample review we created in Chapter 5 looks like this:

```
<?xml version="1.0">
<CYBERCINEMA_REVIEW ID="123">
<HEAD>
...header stuff we're not interested in...
</HEAD>
<BODY>
<!-- Body information goes here -->
The film <MOVIE ID="12345">Spartacus</MOVIE> stars <PERSON ID="932">Tony Curtis</PERSON> as a fun-loving slave. Often confused with
<MOVIE ID="12346">Ben Hur</MOVIE> (see our <REVIEW ID="876">review</REVIEW>),
this 1960's classic is...
</BODY>
</CYBERCINEMA_REVIEW>
```

The decomposition for the PERSON and MOVIE elements were described previously (see the section XML Nitro Injection: Adding Reviews, earlier in this chapter). The decomposition for the REVIEW elements will be quite the same, starting with a relational table:

```
CREATE TABLE review_review (
    review_from_id    INTEGER(16)    NOT NULL    REFERENCES review(review_id),
    review_to_id      INTEGER(16)    NOT NULL    REFERENCES review(review_id),
    PRIMARY KEY (review_from_id, review_to_id)
);
```

The difference is that we're relating from a table back into the same table, so to differentiate the two references, we've labeled them the "from" reference and the "to" reference. In the case of the preceding XML instance, the insert statement performed on decomposition looks like this:

```
INSERT into review_review (review_from_id, review_to_id) VALUES (123, 876);
```

When you're finished, you'll have an exact map of which reviews reference which other reviews. If you decide not to use a review because of a pending lawsuit, the system can quickly and easily tell you which reviews link *to* it.

Selecting What You Need

After you've inserted a few hundred reviews, you'll be able to get your database to respond to fairly specific requests, such as list reviews of movies made between 1990 and 1995 by a certain reviewer where a certain actor was mentioned.

```
SELECT review.id, review.review_xml
FROM review, review_person, person AS reviewer,
    review_movie, movie, movie_person_role, person_role,
    role, person AS actor
WHERE review.review_id = review_person.review_id
AND reviewer.person_id = review_person.person_id
AND review_movie.review_id = review.review_id
AND movie.movie_id = review_movie.movie_id
AND movie.movie_id = movie_person_role.movie_id
AND person_role.person_role_id = movie_person_rolc.person_role_id
AND role.role_id = person_role.role_id
AND actor.person_id = person_role.person_id
AND movie.movie_date > '1990-12-31'
AND movie.movie_date < '1995-01-01'
AND reviewer.person_name LIKE '%Ebert%'
AND role.role_name = 'Actor'
AND actor.person_name = 'Alec Baldwin';
```

The database can reliably answer our request; why you would *want* to ask this request is another issue.

As a bonus, we've also addressed the dead link issue. Because all the links between your documents are mirrored in a database that enforces the integrity of that structure, it's much more difficult to have a bad link. If an author tries to insert a link to a nonexistent movie or review, the database rejects it because it will breach relational integrity to do so. Your authoring interface should give the author some kind of helpful error message, such as "the requested link target does not exist." Again, this leverages the power of the relational database. You won't have to do as much link checking if you know that your database is humming away in the background, ensuring the integrity of your intradocument links.

Using Link Management to Help Power Suggestions

So, after you've developed this elegant database schema around your data, what else can you do with it? Remember when I was spouting off about "emergent properties" of systems in the Introduction? A database schema based on the idea of partial decomposition can also exhibit emergent properties, developing smarts beyond the original design. A good example of this is in the field of suggestions. The complex maps you've built in the review_movie, review_review, and review_person tables can be even more useful, especially if you're interested in making *suggestions* to users, that is, providing information they might be interested in based on what they're looking at now.

The science of suggesting relevant information is nothing new. Many software systems do this through methods such as collaborative filtering or lexical analysis.

The idea behind lexical analysis systems is to break documents down to their lexical components—words or phrases—and compare new documents based on a statistical relevance ranking of these components. In theory, documents that have similar subject matter should rank closely together; in reality, lexical analysis often groups documents that don't necessarily go together.

For instance, lexical engines can readily group all of Shakespeare's works together, but a lexical system can't differentiate between a comedy and a tragedy. If you were reading *Troilus and Cressida* and you wanted the system to show you "more plays like this one," it probably could manage to rule out *Speed the Plow*, but you might just as easily be shown *As You Like It* as *Romeo and Juliet*. The system needs more information than purely lexical similarity to guide it.

Likewise, collaborative filtering, when left to its own devices, can develop strange behaviors. Collaborative filtering attempts to suggest items to you based on matching your own likes and dislikes against all other users on the system. Collaborative filtering's answer to the previous user request involves a complex equation based on what other readers who had read *Troilus and Cressida* had read and enjoyed. This means that you might get a list of other Shakespearean tragedies as well as Greek tragedies and other similar fare. Collaborative filtering misses any advantage it could gain from the content itself, however. You might as well be reading *Dick and Jane*—or eating avocados for that matter. Collaborative filtering system knows only about user responses.

Both lexical analysis and collaborative filtering lack a means to receive editorial input into the suggestion process. If, in the editorial notes for *Troilus and Cressida*, a discussion of Shakespeare's possible influences for this work and his similar works is included, and this discussion includes links to those other works, we now have something to work with. Instead of having to infer the relationships between documents by essentially throwing a dart at a board, the system has hard data about these relationships. It can use lexical analysis or collaborative filtering (or both) to supplement this hard data and give the user access to a richer experience.

In reality, especially in systems with lots of legacy information, hard data about the relationships between documents isn't always possible to get, but when this data is available, you should leverage it—and hard. If your database schema is built correctly and you've used the tools of link management and partial decomposition, you already have a mechanism to manage these types of relationships between documents and to use them to best effect. Your database now knows more about the relationships between your documents than you do because it knows all of the links between documents or from documents to other entities (movies, actors, directors, and so on). However, you have to manage the data input process very closely; otherwise, as they say in the biz, "garbage in, garbage out" will rule the day.

The key is in correctly building the input tools for your internal user base. For example, at CyberCinema, it might be useful to have two kinds of links between articles: One kind might be "related reviews based on topic" (such as "Academy Award nominees for 2001"), and the other might be "related reviews, based on genre" (such as "science fiction" or "Chinese films"). In both cases, you're relating one film review to another but for different reasons. You want to be able to store those links, but also you also want to be able to store the accompanying data of why those links exist. What's the *semantic* value of that link?

An effort is currently underway within the hallowed halls of the World Wide Web Consortium (W3C) to build an XML-based language to address just this problem. The language is called RDF (Resource Description Framework), and its stated goal is to build a new "semantic Web," a Web composed of intelligent links that encode their own raison d'être. It's a splendid goal, but reaching it probably is way in the future. To read more about RDF, visit W3C's RDF pages at http://www.w3.org/RDF/. Tim Bray has written an excellent primer at http://www.xml.com/pub/a/98/06/rdf.html.

In the meantime, you can build your own semantically encoded links using the tools of XLink and partial decomposition. First, let's take our XLink example from Chapter 5 and add optional attributes:

```
<!ELEMENT review ANY>
<!ATTLIST review
    xlink:type       (simple|extended|locator|arc)
                                                    #FIXED "locator"
    <!-- This is a locator link because it points to an external
         resource -->
    xlink:href       CDATA                          #REQUIRED
    xlink:type       (topic | genre | other)        "other"
    xlink:show       (new | embed | replace)        "replace"
    <!-- When link is actuated (such as with a click) should the linked-to
         data come up in a new window, be embedded in the current window or
         replace the current content? -->
    xlink:actuate    (onRequest |onLoad)            "onRequest"
    <!-- How should the link be activated? Default is on user request
         (for example, the user clicks on the link text) -->
>
```

Now let's imagine the following partial decomposition table in which to store this link data:

```
CREATE TABLE review_review (
    review_review_id      INTEGER(16)    NOT NULL    PRIMARY KEY,
    review_review_type    INTEGER(16)    NOT NULL    REFERENCES
                          link_type(link_type_id),
review_from_id            INTEGER(16)    NOT NULL    REFERENCES
                          review(review_id),
    review_to_id          INTEGER(16)    NOT NULL    REFERENCES
                          review(review_id)
);

CREATE TABLE link_type (
    link_type_id    INTEGER(16)    NOT NULL    PRIMARY KEY,
    link_type_name  VARCHAR(16)    NOT NULL
);
```

In this example, we're assuming the link_type table is populated with all possible reasons why something would link to something else. With this arrangement, the database can tell us which review-to-review links are included because of the film's genre and which are included because the films are related by topic. Simply query the database like so:

```
SELECT review_review_id
    WHERE review_review.review_review_type = 1
    AND review_review.review_from_id = 127;
```

Assuming the link_type_id of genre links is "1," you've just selected all genre-type links to other reviews from review 127. You can do something fun with this data such as format all these links in a separate box on the right side of your page (assuming you're formatting a page).

Link Semantics: Making It Easy for Content Creators

Adding semantic information to your links can be powerful, but remember, it requires human intervention to do it correctly. If your content creators aren't required to take the extra step to input this data or if they don't see the benefit, they won't do it. Here are a couple of ideas for easing (encouraging) them to add semantic information:

1. Make your content entry interface easy to use, which usually means making use of interface elements (such as checkboxes, radio buttons, and so forth).
2. Make it impossible for your content authors to skip steps. Doing this means they are shown a warning dialog box or a message stating that they have to fill in certain fields before the system will let them save their content. The disadvantage of doing this is that your content authors will find it annoying and will find ways to subvert it. For instance, if the system requires them to enter an expected publish date in order to "file" an article, the content authors might enter any old date in order to file the article. If the system is too restrictive, they just won't use it. You can build the most full-featured workflow system in the world, but if it isn't easy to use and if your content authors don't think it makes their jobs easier, they will subvert it.
3. The best way to encourage content authors to add semantic information is to make the benefit of extra content entry visible to the author, as in an earlier example where I recommended moving the links relating to genre into a separate box on the side of the article. Content authors usually care about these types of features because readers care about them. Content editors, or managers in charge of content, really care about them. If your content authoring interface enables authors to put their links into a special box, that's a feature, not an added annoyance.

Unfortunately, there's no good way to force content authors to input semantic data or metadata for which they don't see tangible benefit. This is where those poor interns come in handy.

Summary

If you take nothing else away from this chapter, remember the principles of partial decomposition:

- XML instances are stored whole somewhere (I recommend in the database itself).
- Selected information that's important for your application is extracted from the XML into relational tables.
- The relational tables are updated whenever (and only when) an XML file is updated (or inserted), thereby keeping XML in the driver's seat.
- By enforcing relational constraints, the database enforces data integrity in and between your XML files.
- Your application will generally use the information in the relational tables to answer requests about your data (like "list all reviews by a certain author"). Because integrity has been enforced, your application can rely on the database to respond *accurately* to these requests.
- When you want to display or otherwise convert an XML instance, grab the whole instance from the database.

Partial decomposition is a tool that I've found useful across a range of applications. It's simple, it's easy to build in a "componentized" fashion, and it powerfully combines the best of XML with the best of SQL.

At this point, we've covered the XML application development life cycle from requirements definition, through data modeling, XML design, and database schema design. The next step is to build your application— actually to write application code in your platform of choice, be that Perl, Java, VisualBasic, object-oriented Fortran, or whatever. The building of your application is beyond the scope of this book, although we'll discuss some aspects of it in Chapters 8 and 9. With a foundation built on the topics we've covered thus far, however, the task of writing your application will be much easier.

In the next chapters, we'll discuss some other XML standards that can be powerful tools when developing XML applications, and we'll discuss two frameworks (Sun's Java 2 Enterprise Edition and Microsoft's SQL Server 2000) for building those applications. Finally, we'll cover some further examples of how to integrate SQL and XML. Throughout, we'll be applying the principals discussed here and in the previous chapters, such as partial decomposition.

Chapter 7

Related Standards: XSLT, XML Schema, and Other Flora and Fauna

> In which XML is magically transformed, and
> the XPath to righteousness is revealed!

The development of XML has spawned a shadow industry of XML-based languages, each developed and promoted by its own industry group or consortium. Many of these standards seem to conflict with each other or with products that are already widely in use. Untangling it to find the right standard to apply to a particular problem can be, well, problematic.

In this chapter, I discuss some of the standards that I've found particularly useful in designing and building applications with XML and SQL. You'll discover how to transform your XML with XSLT and why XML Schema is fast becoming a replacement for XML DTDs. I'll also cover some approaches to querying XML documents and touch on the XPath, an important standard for referring to parts of XML documents.

As a rule of thumb, anything produced under the auspices of the W3C is going to be a relevant and utilized standard. Of course, the W3C devotes resources only to efforts that it considers "general" enough. So, for instance, the W3C has devoted quite a lot of effort to developing and promoting XML, but it doesn't get involved in efforts such as producing an XML vocabulary specific to news articles or other knowledge domains. The W3C develops the standards (such as XML) that enable these more domain-specific languages. An abundance of these domain-specific languages is available, covering fields from chemical formulas to legal contracts. Information on them can be found in the sites listed at the end of Chapter 5.

The standards discussed in this chapter are important tools that you should be familiar with when building any XML application.

XSLT: XML Transformers!

Once you're in XML land, 80 percent of what your applications will do involves converting one type of XML to another. For instance, your domain-specific language (our movie review XML format) will have to be converted into many different XHTML (XML-compliant HTML) variants for different versions of Web sites (which you might need if you were supporting many types of browsers on many types of devices), including Wireless Markup Language (WML, another XML derivative) for delivery to WAP phones. In addition, the domain-specific language may be packaged for syndication with the Information Content Exchange (ICE) language (again, XML-derived) or converted into another data exchange language and so forth and so on. One immensely useful and exciting standard developed by the W3C is the Extensible Style Language or XSL and its derivative language, XSLT or XSL Transformation. XML processors based on the XSLT grammar can be used to convert (transform) between different XML-based languages quickly and easily.

Regular Expressions

At times you may be tempted to use *regular expressions* to transform bits of XML into other bits of XML. Regular expressions are essentially markup language for describing strings that enable you to search for and replace them in documents. For instance, the regular expression `/foo/` searches for the string "foo" wherever it occurs in whatever is being searched.

It's especially tempting to make use of regular expressions in scripting languages such as Perl, which makes it almost impossible *not* to use them. Although the XML community generally turns up its nose at regular expressions, I have found it useful to make use of regular expressions for transformation of XML in limited cases.

Regular expressions have the advantage of being fast; you don't need a parser, a tree, an object model, or anything like that. When you use regular expressions to convert XML, you're *not guaranteed* to get valid XML on the output side, which can cause problems that you might not even discover until months after a system is operational.

A good rule of thumb for the use of regular expressions is to ask yourself, "Will anything ever parse or otherwise attempt to treat the output of what I'm converting as an XML document?" If so, I strongly recommend that you not use regular expressions and use the more heavyweight but reliable XSLT engines. *Learn from my mistakes*! The bother you think you're saving yourself now by using regular expressions will revisit you tenfold when you find that half the XML in your database is corrupt, unparsable garbage. Hey, don't say I didn't warn you.

If, however, you're converting bits of XML into bits of some other data-exchange language (such as EDI or a messaging system like MQ Series), regular expressions might be your ticket. XSLT *can* do this kind of conversion, but regular expressions may be faster and more efficient.

Transformation has always been a huge part of dealing with SGML and XML-based languages at the server side. This process usually consists of building a rule-based transformation script that acts within an XML parser to execute the transition. I remember writing this sort of script within a Perl-based parser back in 1995; there's nothing amazingly new about transformations of this kind. There's an important difference with XSL Transformations: XSLT can be described as XML Transformation via example. You feed a source XML file and an XSLT template into an XSLT processor, and the processor does the work of figuring out how to build the transform. (The XSLT template shows the XSLT processor how you want your result document to appear.)

So How Does XSLT Work Exactly?

Let's begin to examine XSLT with a very brief example. The following is a simple XSL Transformation (XSLT) template:

```
<xsl:transform>
  <xsl:template match="ABSTRACT">
    <p><em><xsl:apply-templates/></em></p>
  </xsl:template>
</xsl:transform>
```

This transformation rule looks for any element named "ABSTRACT" and creates, in a result tree, a corresponding element, wrapped in XHTML <p> and <em> tags. So if your original document looked something like this:

```
<CYBERCINEMA_REVIEW ID="1234">
<HEAD>
<!-- Header information goes here -->
<AUTHOR_BLOCK>
<AUTHOR ID="123">Daniel Appelquist</AUTHOR>
</AUTHOR_BLOCK>
<MOVIE ID="3827">Gone With the Wind</MOVIE>
<HEADLINE>Classic Film Still Fresh</HEADLINE>
<ABSTRACT>A <EM>fantastic</EM> film that still holds up after all...</ABSTRACT>
<CREATE_DATE DATE="…"/>
<LASTMOD_DATE DATE="…"/>
<PUBLISH_DATE DATE="…"/>
</HEAD>
<BODY>
<!-- Body information goes here -->
</BODY>
</CYBERCINEMA_REVIEW>
```

Your result document will look like this:

```
<p><em>A <EM>fantastic</EM> film that still holds up after all...</em></p>
```

Because the transformation style sheet doesn't contain rules for any other element, only the abstract (and any nodes underneath it) appears in the result document, wrapped up as specified in the style sheet.

XSLT can also be used to extract elements from XML documents using their XPath designations, to wit:

```
<xsl:transform>
<xsl:template match="/">
<html>
  <head>
    <title>Cyber-Cinema review: <xsl:value-of select="CYBERCINEMA_REVIEW/HEAD/MOVIE"/></title>
  </head>
  <body>
    <h2><xsl:value-of select="CYBERCINEMA_REVIEW/HEAD/MOVIE"/></h2>
    <h3><xsl:value-of select="CYBERCINAMA_REVIEW/HEAD/AUTHOR_BLOCK/AUTHOR"/>
    <p><em><xsl:value-of select="CYBERCINEMA_REVIEW/HEAD/ABSTRACT"/></em></p>
    <hr/>
    <p><xsl:value-of select="CYBERCINEMA_REVIEW/BODY"/></p>
  </body>
</html>
</xsl:template>
<!--the rule to style REVIEW links-->
<xsl:template match="REVIEW">
    <em><xsl:apply-templates/></em>
</xsl:template>
</xsl:transform>
```

Applying this XSLT style sheet to one of our movie reviews results in a fully formed XML result document (in this case, XHTML). As a bonus, because of the previously presented rule that matches on the "REVIEW" tag, every movie review link is styled in *emphasis* in the resulting document.

XPath

XPath (http://www.w3.org/TR/xpath) is a language for addressing parts of an XML document in the same way that a file path (like C:\my_dir\my_file.doc under DOS/Windows or /tmp/textfile.txt under UNIX file systems) addresses a particular file on a file system. It's the basis of expressions within XSLT as well as in a host of other XML languages (such as XQuery, described in the section Querying XML Documents, later in this chapter) that address specific parts of documents. XPath is a grammar for describing the internal structure of XML documents. Taking our movie review document as an example, a location path to the BODY element is

```
/CYBERCINEMA_REVIEW/BODY
```

It seems simple enough. XPath enables you to address nodes within an XML document using a relative syntax, like a file system. The following selects all movies within the node above "current node":

```
../MOVIE
```

You might use this syntax if your code is in the middle of transforming a MOVIE node within your review's BODY and needs to find all other movies referred to from within the review currently being transformed. In this way, XPath has a limited query capability. Although it isn't as robust as XQuery, it may be all you need within your application (for instance, if your XML documents are relatively simple, like the ones we've been discussing in this book).

For more information on XPath, visit the W3C's pages on XPath at http://www.w3.org/TR/xpath.

XSLT's True Life Purpose

XSLT's main purpose is to transform (or convert) between specific XML vocabularies (for example, Newsml, an XML-derived language specific to news stories) and XSL's "formatting object" language. As such, XSLT is really not intended by its creators for use as a general-purpose XML transformation engine.

XSL defines a generic formatting language, with tags that start with the prefix `<fo:`. Each tag represents a particular formatting characteristic (for example, visual characteristics such as color, alignment, font size, and font face and also aural characteristics such as pitch and tone for text-to-speech processors). XSL is an industrial-strength formatting language that promises to play a huge part in the

way information is *presented* to the user. A discussion of the specifics of XSL are a bit out of scope in this book.

Even though XSLT's stated purpose is specifically to be used within the XSL formatting language, it's a great tool for transforming between different XML vocabularies as well.

For more information, visit the W3C's page on XSL at http://www.w3.org/TR/xsl/.

XML Schema: An Alternative to DTDs

XML Schema is an alternative and, some say, a better way to define the structure and content of XML documents. XML Schema actually goes way beyond the DTD by defining not only the legal ordering and nesting of tags but also the content types (integer, character, string, and so forth) associated with those tags. XML Schema brings XML closer to what relational databases can do by enabling you to have rigidly defined types.

As of this writing, XML Schema is gaining acceptance in the XML community, and more software is starting to support it, but it is still quite young.

DTDs Versus XML Schema

You may ask, "Why did we bother with all that DTD stuff if now you're telling me XML Schema is better?" While XML Schema may supercede XML DTDs as a method of choice for XML design, it's important to understand how DTDs work.

DTDs are a fundamental part of XML. Anything you can design with XML Schema has a corresponding DTD. The DTD still "exists" by definition, even if it isn't documented or written anywhere. The same cannot be said in reverse because some (admittedly obscure) language features of XML can't be modeled with XML Schema.

Depending on the XML tool set you use, you may decide to use XML Schema for your XML design, or you may decide to use good, old, traditional DTDs. Or, as we'll see in Chapter 8, you might decide to use XML Data-Reduced (XDR), which is a Microsoft-proposed alternative to DTDs and XML Schema. Each of these languages is a way to constrain the design of XML documents, and each is appropriate to a particular use.

Let's look at an example that shows how we can construct an XML Schema definition for our CyberCinema example. Alert readers should be familiar with the following XML fragment:

```
<?xml version="1.0">
<CYBERCINEMA_REVIEW ID="123">
<HEAD>
<!-- Header information goes here -->
<AUTHOR_BLOCK>
<AUTHOR ID="123">Daniel Appelquist</AUTHOR>
</AUTHOR_BLOCK>
<MOVIE ID="12345">Spartacus</MOVIE>
<HEADLINE>Roman Holiday</HEADLINE>
<ABSTRACT>Made famous by its chariot race, this film marks the pinnacle of historical action drama.</ABSTRACT>
<CREATE_DATE DATE="…"/>
<LASTMOD_DATE DATE="…"/>
<PUBLISH_DATE DATE="…"/>
</HEAD>
<BODY>
<!-- Body information goes here -->
The film <MOVIE ID="12345">Spartacus</MOVIE> stars <PERSON ID="932">Tony Curtis</PERSON> as a fun-loving slave. Often confused with
<MOVIE ID="12346">Ben Hur</MOVIE> (see our <REVIEW ID="876">review</REVIEW>), this 1960's classic is...
</BODY>
</CYBERCINEMA_REVIEW>
```

The preceding is an example instance of our movie review document format, for which we already created a DTD (see Chapter 5). The equivalent XML Schema definition for the same document type is as follows:

```
<xsd:schema>

 <xsd:annotation>
  <xsd:documentation>
   Movie review Schema for Cybercinema.com.
```

```
      Copyright 2001 Cybercinema.com. All rights reserved.
    </xsd:documentation>
  </xsd:annotation>

<xsd:element name="CYBERCINEMA_REVIEW" type="CYBERCINEMA_REVIEW_TYPE"/>

<xsd:complexType name="CYBERCINEMA_REVIEW_TYPE">
  <xsd:sequence>

    <xsd:element name="HEAD" type="REVIEW_HEAD_TYPE"/>
    <xsd:element name="BODY" type="REVIEW_TEXT_TYPE"/>

  </xsd:sequence>

  <xsd:attribute name="ID" type="xsd:positiveInteger"/>
</xsd:complexType>

<xsd:complexType name="CYBERCINEMA_HEAD_TYPE">
  <xsd:sequence>

    <xsd:element name="AUTHOR_BLOCK" type="AUTHOR_BLOCK_TYPE"/>

    <xsd:element name="MOVIE" type="xsd:string"/>

    <xsd:element name="HEADLINE" type="xsd:string"/>

    <xsd:element name="ABSTRACT" type="REVIEW_TEXT_TYPE"/>

    <xsd:element name="CREATE_DATE">
    <xsd:attribute name="DATE" type="xsd:date"/>
    </xsd:element>

    <xsd:element name="LASTMOD_DATE" type="xsd:date">
    <xsd:attribute name="DATE" type="xsd:date"/>
    </xsd:element>
```

```
         <xsd:element name="PUBLISH_DATE" type="xsd:date">
         <xsd:attribute name="DATE" type="xsd:date"/>
         </xsd:element>

    </xsd:sequence>
</xsd:complexType>

<xsd:complexType name="AUTHOR_BLOCK_TYPE">
 <xsd:sequence>

    <xsd:element name="AUTHOR"
                 minOccurs="1"
                 maxOccurs="unbounded"
                 type="xsd:string"/>
      <name="ID" type="xsd:positiveInteger"/>
    </xsd:element>

 </xsd:sequence>
</xsd:complexType>

 <xsd:complexType name="REVIEW_TEXT_TYPE" mixed="true">
    <xsd:all>

      <xsd:element name="MOVIE" type="xsd:LINK_TYPE"/>

      <xsd:element name="PERSON" type="xsd:LINK_TYPE"/>

      <xsd:element name="REVIEW" type=" xsd:LINK_TYPE"/>

    </xsd:all>
 </xsd:complexType>

 <xsd:simpleType name="LINK_TYPE" type="xsd:string">
    <xsd:attribute name="ID" type="xsd:positiveInteger"/>
 </xsd:simpleType>

</xsd:schema>
```

This example includes a definition of elements (much as in a DTD, except with the syntax <xsd:element…>) and simple types and complex types for each of these elements (defined with the syntax <xsd:simpleType…> or <xsd:complexType…>). Each of these types enables you to define the content models and attribute lists as defined in our DTD. For example, in CYBERCINEMA_REVIEW_TYPE, we define that the contents of the tag are a fixed sequence of first a HEAD tag and then a BODY tag. Then we define with the <xsd:attribute…> syntax that this tag should have an ID field. The major advantage is that, with an XML Schema, we can use data typing (the ability to use data types such as integers and strings). I can define my ID elements as being positive integers (as I have done for the ID numbers by using type="xsd:positiveInteger"). I can identify date elements as dates (as I have done with the dates in this example by using type="xsd:date" in the attribute definitions). The idea of typing is a whole new world for XML document definition. Data typing in an XML Schema file and the corresponding tools that support XML Schemas give you the ability to check and enforce these types, which brings XML one step closer to SQL. The <xsd:annotation> element at the top of the example is an annotation for a comment.

You can also specify allowed recurrence of items. For example, in the AUTHOR_BLOCK type that I defined earlier, I use minOccurs="1" to specify that there must be a minimum of one author and use maxOccurs="unbounded" to specify that there is no maximum to the number of authors allowed.

In my REVIEW_TEXT_TYPE, all I needed to do was add mixed=true in the type definition to specify that this type allows text and tags to be mixed, and the designation <xsd:all> indicates that any of the list of elements specified therein (MOVIE, PERSON, and REVIEW) are legal tags to appear within the text.

A host of tools and material is available on the use of XML Schema in real-life XML application development. Major tool vendors such IBM, Microsoft, and Oracle, as well as some less well-known industry heavyweights such as SAP and TIBCO, have lined up behind it.

The main page for XML Schemas (http://www.w3.org/XML/schema) contains a Tools section that lists many free and open-source implementations of XML Schema, as well as XML Schema conversion and validation tools to make your life easier. Another fantastic resource for XML Schemas is XML.com's tutorial, which can be found at http://www.xml.com/pub/a/2000/11/29/schemas/part1.html.

In building systems with XML and SQL, when you're using XML Schema for your XML files, it's important to make sure your database schema supports all the features specified in your XML Schema. For instance, if your XML Schema specifies that author names can be 50 characters long (as may be done with a `<xsd:maxLength value="50"/>` tag in the type definition), then your database had better support at least 50 characters. When you use XML Schema, you will probably be transferring some of the responsibility for enforcing restrictions like this from the database to an XML Schema-compliant XML processor, so be extra careful about synchronizing these restrictions between your XML Schema and your database.

Querying XML Documents

Much of what we've been discussing in this book is strategies to allow you to query collections of XML instances using a SQL database. Almost all of Chapter 6 is devoted to this topic. There is another approach to getting information out of individual XML instances and collections of XML instances, using new querying standards that are either fresh out of development or still in development. These new standards promise to bring new options to the developer who will be building the kinds of systems we've been discussing in this book.

XPath, which we already discussed in this chapter (see the sidebar XPath) is a simple means to query information within an XML instance. As we'll see in Chapter 8, Microsoft also makes use of the XPath standard in their SQL Server 2000 product as a query mechanism for XML. XPath is all about looking at a single XML instance, however. There are two leading contenders for a standard, more robust querying specification for collections of XML instances: XML Query and SQLX.

XML Query

The W3C has released the XQuery specification (http://www.w3.org/XML/query), which promises to enable the querying of XML documents in the same way that you can query a SQL database. Here's an example of XQuery syntax applicable to our review document:

```
document("review1.xml")/BODY/REVIEW
```

This XQuery statement returns all the reviews referred to in the body of the XML document review1.xml.

The syntax of the XQuery language is built around the XPath representation of XML data structures. The XQuery language also provides for complex instructions within queries. For instance, you process through a corpus of XML documents, returning the titles and abstracts only for those that meet a certain set of criteria. This functionality mirrors that of SQL in many ways. In fact, not satisfied with simply querying within XML documents, the XQuery folks are also attacking the problem of how to query SQL databases using XQuery. This might seem like reinventing the wheel, but the thrust of the argument is this: Why have one query language for relational databases and another query language for XML documents when you can have a single query language that does both? Using one language simplifies development, architecture, and the modeling of data.

The usual cast of characters (Microsoft, Oracle, Sun, and so forth) are in the working group, so there's every chance XQuery will be adopted by many vendors of XML and relational tools and applications. However, as of this writing, it hasn't yet been adopted.

SQLX: The Truth Is Out There

A few small companies (most notably Microsoft, Oracle, and—surprise, surprise—IBM) are implementing an effort to bridge the gap between SQL and XML. These shadowy figures that meet in darkened, smoke-filled rooms are quite adept at keeping their purpose well concealed. Indeed, at this writing their Web site (http://www.sqlx.org) provides only cryptic clues as to their intent. My informant (we'll call him "Deep Throat") informs me that their goal is to build standard extensions on top of SQL to query XML documents within relational databases.

In all seriousness, SQLX is an effort you should watch. As opposed to the XQuery effort, which asks "How can we create a single XML-based query language?" SQLX is approaching the problem from the angle of "How do we adapt SQL to include XML documents?" If these extensions are ratified by international standards bodies and become part of the major database products, they could start a revolution in the way XML is managed within these widely deployed database packages, rendering some of the information in this book obsolete.

Summary

In this chapter, I've touched on the other important standards and their importance in building systems with XML and SQL. These standards are constantly evolving, just as XML and SQL are, although at a slower pace. Keeping up with them can sometimes feel like a full-time job. You'll get halfway to developing an XML-derived language some time in your career, only to discover that it's already been developed by someone else. The way to avoid that happening is to frequent sites like www.w3.org, www.xml.com, and www.xml.org.

Chapter 8

XML and SQL Server 2000

In which an old dog learns some new tricks.

Throughout this book I've talked about XML and relational databases and how the two technologies are related. In this chapter, I want to take you down one more level and look at some specific ways in which XML and relational databases can be highly integrated. I'm going to use Microsoft SQL Server 2000 as an example of one of many available relational database servers that ship with features that provide many ways to integrate XML documents with relational databases. So put on your greasy overalls because we're going to take a look under the hood and poke around an XML-friendly database engine.

SQL Server 2000 has features not only for storing XML documents but also for processing and querying XML documents at the database server, without the need for external components. It also supports various ways of formatting queries in XML. I'll discuss some scenarios where these features are most appropriate, as well as some scenarios where other options may be more advantageous. First, I briefly want to introduce the main XML features of SQL Server 2000.

The features boil down to three major categories of functionality:

- **Retrieve data in XML format.** With SQL Server you can issue queries and receive results formatted in XML. You can even control the format of the results through various means. You're not limited to issuing SQL queries; you can query relational databases with the XML query language XPath.
- **Work with XML documents on the database server.** In addition to formatting query results in XML, you can also work directly with XML documents on the database server. You can even use the data in XML documents to populate and modify data in your relational databases.
- **Communicate with SQL Server over the Internet and intranets.** SQL Server provides a way to access your databases over the Web through a variety of techniques that we'll discuss. Some of the methods of access even use XML to format commands sent to SQL Server over the Web. This feature can make your data available to applications regardless of the platforms they run on or the language they're written in.

Throughout this chapter, I'll describe these features and show you how you can use them. However, this chapter is intended to give you a taste of what you can do with XML and relational database servers—specifically, with SQL Server 2000. An entire book could be written on the XML features of SQL Server alone, so this chapter does not attempt to cover every feature or explore any of the features in great depth. Instead, I hope that you come away from this chapter with concrete knowledge of how XML and SQL can be married in a powerful way at the level of a relational database server. You can apply this knowledge to your own projects, using either SQL Server 2000 or some other relational database server, such as Oracle, that might have similar features.

Retrieving Data in XML Format

SQL Server 2000 provides several ways to retrieve data in XML format from SQL Server. You can retrieve XML data through normal database connections or across a HyperText Transfer Protocol (HTTP) connection, such as an intranet or even the Internet. When connecting over HTTP, you can even use

XML to communicate with the database server, in addition to getting results formatted in XML. First, I want to show you how to retrieve data formatted in XML, regardless of how you're connecting to your database or the format of your queries.

FOR XML

SQL Server 2000 adds to the SELECT statement a new clause, called the FOR XML clause, which instructs SQL Server to return the result of a query in XML format. You even have control over the format of the XML returned. The easiest way to understand how this feature works is to look at an example.

Suppose you were working with the Northwind database that ships with SQL Server, and you wanted to see the names of the customers who live in Germany. Customer information in the Northwind database is stored in a table called Customers. Normally you would issue the following query to return this result set:

```
SELECT ContactName
FROM Customers
WHERE Country = 'Germany'
```

To return the results in XML format, you simply change this code by adding the FOR XML clause, along with at least one argument that I'll explain shortly.

```
SELECT ContactName
FROM Customers
WHERE Country = 'Germany'
FOR XML RAW
```

This query returns the following results (only the first few rows are shown for brevity):

```
  <row ContactName="Maria Anders" />
  <row ContactName="Hanna Moos" />
  <row ContactName="Sven Ottlieb" />
  ...
```

By simply adding "FOR XML RAW," SQL Server returned the results in XML format. If you have access to SQL Server 2000, you can issue this same query on the Northwind database, and you'll see the same results, providing you haven't modified the database.

The last part of the FOR XML clause shown indicates the mode, or format, of the returned XML content. For this example, I chose the RAW mode, which simply returns each row in an element named row, and columns of the row are returned as attributes of the element.

FOR XML AUTO

Two other modes, AUTO and EXPLICIT, are available. The mode AUTO tells SQL Server to produce some additional information about our results in the returned XML content. Consider the differences between the use of the RAW mode in the preceding example and the use of the AUTO mode in the following example:

```
SELECT ContactName
FROM Customers
WHERE Country = 'Germany'
FOR XML AUTO
```

This query produces the following XML output:

```
<customers ContactName="Maria Anders" />
<customers ContactName="Hanna Moos" />
<customers ContactName="Sven Ottlieb" />
...
```

In this case, SQL Server names each row element with the name of the table in the result set. Again, columns from the table are returned as attributes. What happens if we return columns from more than one table? Suppose we want to see a list of customers and all of the orders each customer has placed.

```
SELECT ContactName, OrderID
FROM Customers
```

```
   INNER JOIN Orders ON Customers.CustomerID = Orders.OrderID
WHERE Customers.Country = 'Germany'
FOR XML AUTO
```

This query returns the following XML results:

```
<customers ContactName="Maria Anders">
  <orders OrderID="10643" />
  <orders OrderID="10692" />
   …
  </customers>
<customers ContactName="Hanna Moos">
  <orders OrderID="10501" />
  <orders OrderID="10509" />
   …
  </customers>
<customers ContactName="Sven Ottlieb">
  <orders OrderID="10363" />
   …
```

As you can see, the inner table row elements were returned as children of the outer table's elements. So all of the orders for each customer are listed as child rows of the corresponding customer.

FOR XML EXPLICIT

I'm not going to discuss the third mode, EXPLICIT, thoroughly because it is a lengthy topic, the details are beyond the scope of this book, and I don't necessarily recommend using it unless you find a really good reason to use it. This mode gives you more explicit control over the format of the XML output returned in response to queries. For example, if you wish to format the results of a query to conform to a complicated XML schema that represents a purchase order document that you use to communicate with e-commerce trading partners, an XML document produced with the RAW or AUTO formats probably won't suffice. You could still use those formats and transform the results into your purchase order document format, programmatically or with XSLT transformations. Or you could choose to use the EXPLICIT mode and format them as they're returned from SQL Server. It can be quite cumbersome to format queries using the EXPLICIT mode. Later, for retrieving XML results from SQL Server, I'll show you a different method that can be a useful alternative to the EXPLICIT mode of the FOR XML clause.

Communicating with SQL Server over the Web

The FOR XML clause can be issued from traditional means of connecting to SQL Server, such as through the SQL Server Query Analyzer or programmatically through standard database libraries like ADO for Windows platforms and JDBC for Java. However, each of the remaining methods of access require a different form of communication. To issue a query with the other methods requires communication through the protocol of the Web, HTTP. Therefore, before I go on to describe other ways in which you can query a database and receive XML data in response, let me diverge a bit and describe how to Web-enable SQL Server databases.

HTTP is the standard protocol that Web browsers and Web servers use to communicate across the World Wide Web and across intranets. However, its use is not limited to Web browsers; any client application may communicate with a Web server providing it can speak HTTP. Many libraries are available, both at no cost and for sale, that provide prebuilt components for communicating with HTTP. In fact, Web browsers are just another client application running on a computer that uses some HTTP library to communicate with Web servers.

Some of you may already be jumping out of your socks wondering why anyone in his right mind would ever expose his database server to "direct" access over the Internet. While it's healthy to be paranoid when it comes to protecting databases, there are a couple of things you should know before you run screaming from the room. First, these features work just as well for an intranet application as they do for an Internet or extranet application. Second, access to the database server is not direct. Microsoft Internet Information Server (IIS) handles all of the direct communication with the outside world. So you can still use these features in the context of common network security schemes just as you would with any other database application with a Web server front end. Throughout this section, I'll point out some specific security concerns as they arise, and I'll mention some ways you can mitigate the risks. For now, please put your socks back on and keep reading. These features are powerful when used properly.

Under the Hood

The architecture of the SQL Server 2000 extensions for IIS is straightforward. Figure 8-1 shows a simplified diagram of the architecture.

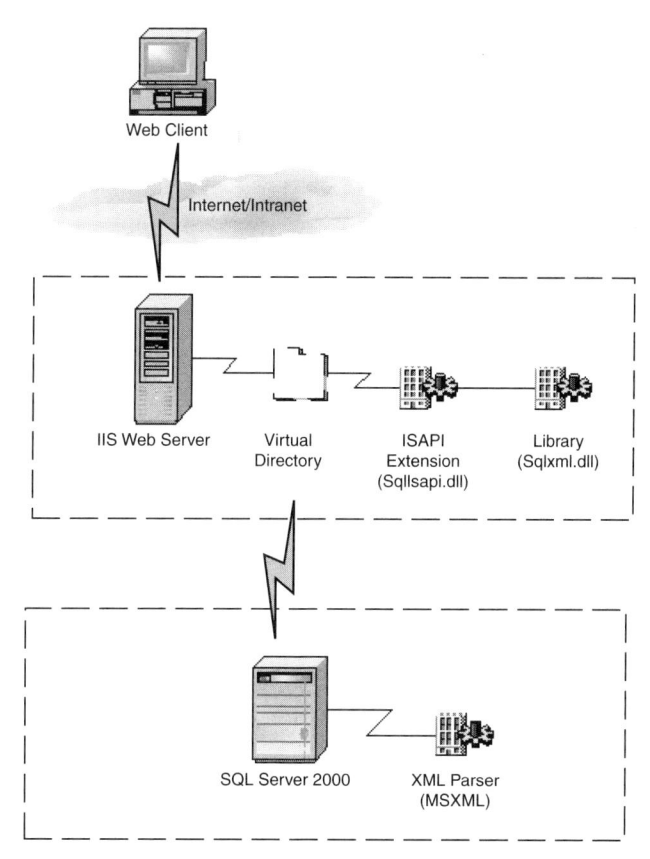

Figure 8-1: Simplified view of the SQL Server 2000 XML architecture

Breaking down the diagram in Figure 8-1, Web clients, be they Web browsers or custom applications, send an HTTP request to a special directory on the IIS Web server. This directory is known as a *virtual directory*. It is just a path that can be accessed on the Web server and that points to a different physical path on the file system. However, this virtual directory must be one that was configured by the administrator specifically to handle SQL Server requests. Administrators configure this type of virtual directory using a configuration tool that Microsoft provides. This virtual directory maps to a special ISAPI (Internet Server API) library (Sqlisapi.dll), installed with SQL Server 2000, that knows how to handle SQL Server requests sent to the Web server.

The ISAPI library processes the request initially and then hands the request to another library (Sqlxml.dll), which processes the request and translates it into specific instructions for SQL Server. As you'll learn, a client can make several different types of requests to SQL Server; some of them may involve some processing steps before the statement is actually sent to SQL Server. Once processed, the statement is passed to SQL Server for execution.

If the statements sent contain the FOR XML clause, which you've already learned about, or the OPENXML clause, which we'll discuss later in the chapter, SQL Server itself executes those statements and may generate XML. After SQL Server generates a result, it returns the result to the calling application.

I've presented a simplified description of the architecture here, but it should give you a good idea of how clients communicate with SQL Server as well as where individual pieces of a request are processed.

Retrieving Data in XML Format—Continued

Now that you know you can communicate with SQL Server over HTTP, let's look at the remaining ways in which you can query SQL Server from across an intranet or the Internet and receive results formatted in XML.

> In certain cases, you can query SQL Server and receive results as an unformatted stream of concatenated strings instead of XML. You can read more about this option in SQL Server Books Online (available for download on Microsoft's site—see http://www.microsoft.com/sql/techinfo/productdoc/ 2000/).

SQL Queries in URLs

You can directly issue SQL queries in the query string of a URL. The URL must point to the virtual directory that points to SQL Server discussed earlier. You must specify the FOR XML clause in the query if you want the results to be returned as XML.

> Using a browser that is capable of interpreting and rendering XML, such as Internet Explorer 5 and above, you can directly view the XML results of queries sent by way of a URL in the browser. Previewing results in a browser is an easy way to test and debug the connection to a database.

URLs must be formatted according to a particular syntax so that Web servers know how to parse their contents. This syntax includes requirements to encode spaces and other special characters with other characters that are legal in a URL. This is known as *URL encoding*. A space, for example, must be encoded as a plus sign (+) or its ASCII equivalent value in hexadecimal. For instance, suppose you wanted to send the following query in a URL:

```
SELECT ContactName FROM Customers FOR XML AUTO
```

Look at how this query would be encoded when sent in the query string of a URL. In this example, the URL refers to a SQL Server that has a registered virtual directory mypath on the IIS server named my server.

```
http://myserver/mypath?sql=SELECT+ContactName+FROM+Customers+FOR+XML+AUTO
```

Alternately, the URL can be expressed with illegal values encoded in hexadecimal notation. With this method, illegal characters are converted into their ASCII value, in hexadecimal, and the percent sign (%) is added as a prefix. Using this notation, the same query looks like the following:

```
http://localhost/nwind?sql=SELECT%20ContactName%20FROM%20Customers%20FOR%20XML%20AUTO
```

In order to try this feature and preview the results in Internet Explorer, you'll need to enclose the results in a root element; otherwise, Internet Explorer reports an error. You can do this by passing another parameter to the URL query string specifying the name of the root element. Parameters in URL query strings are sent as name/value pairs. In URLs, name/value pairs are separated by an ampersand character (&). Altering the preceding query, the proper form of the URL for previewing in Internet Explorer is the following:

```
http://myserver/mypath?sql=SELECT+ContactName+FROM+Customers+FOR+
XML+AUTO&root=ROOT
```

You don't have to name your root element "ROOT." You can call it Ray, or you can call it Jay, or you can even call it RayJay if you want (no spaces).

Encoding lengthy or complex queries, such as queries that contain subqueries, can be cumbersome, as you can see. Fortunately, less awkward alternatives actually use XML to format queries sent to SQL Server.

A word of caution regarding this feature is warranted. Opening your server to the Internet (or even an intranet) and enabling any user who can find your server to execute any query is a dangerous power to enable. The SQL Server configuration tool for configuring the SQL Server virtual directory provides security settings for enabling or disabling URL queries. You should consider disabling URL queries on production systems, given the immense security risk. On development systems, the feature can be useful for testing and debugging.

Template Files

Templates are XML representations of queries stored in a file. You can also call stored procedures from a template. Templates can be sent in URLs in a fashion similar to sending SQL queries in URLs, or templates can be stored in files on the same Web server as the virtual directory that points to SQL Server. Template queries can be executed simply by referencing the name of the template file and the name of the special subdirectory where all templates are held in the URL. For example, the following template query executes the query stored in the file MyTemplate.xml:

```
http://myserver/mypath/templates/MyTemplate.xml
```

Using template files is one way to avoid the hassle of URL encoding your queries. Even though queries are predefined in the template file, the template may specify parameters, and values may be passed in the calling URL for those parameters. The syntax for defining template queries is relatively simple, and the schema is defined in the documentation that ships with SQL Server. An example will demonstrate the basic idea.

Suppose I want to issue the following SQL query against the Northwind database that ships with SQL Server and receive XML results in return.

```
SELECT ContactName
FROM Customers
WHERE Country=@Country
FOR XML Auto
```

I construct the following template file and format my query in XML as shown:

```
<ROOT xmlns:sql="urn:schemas-microsoft-com:xml-sql">
   <sql:header>
      <sql:param name="Country">Germany</sql:param>
   </sql:header>

   <sql:query>
        SELECT ContactName
        FROM Customers
        WHERE Country=@Country
        FOR XML Auto
   </sql:query>
</ROOT>
```

Then I save this file in a subdirectory of the special virtual directory that points to SQL Server. The subdirectory must be one I've configured to hold templates.

The XML schema for templates is fairly simple and is fully defined in the SQL Server Books Online documentation. One nice thing about XML is that it is self-documenting. You should have no trouble reading this code and figuring out what the various pieces represent. One thing that might not be obvious is the data between the starting and ending sql:param tags. This data represents the default value for the parameter, Country, if no parameter is specified by the caller. Queries with parameters do not have to specify a default value; although if it is unspecified, the query fails when the caller does not specify a value for the parameter in the call.

To fire this query and get the results, I simply type the following URL into Internet Explorer (version 5 or above):

```
http://localhost/nwind/template/select1.xml
```

This returns the names of all customers from Germany because I did not specify a value for the Country parameter in the URL. I can specify a parameter to the query by simply adding a name/value pair to the URL where the name is the same name as the parameter defined in the template file:

```
http://localhost/nwind/template/select1.xml?Country=USA
```

The results are returned to Internet Explorer, which formats them nicely in the content pane of the browser as shown in Figure 8-2.

Template files are more secure than SQL queries sent by means of a URL in at least two ways. First, since you predefine queries in a file and these files reside

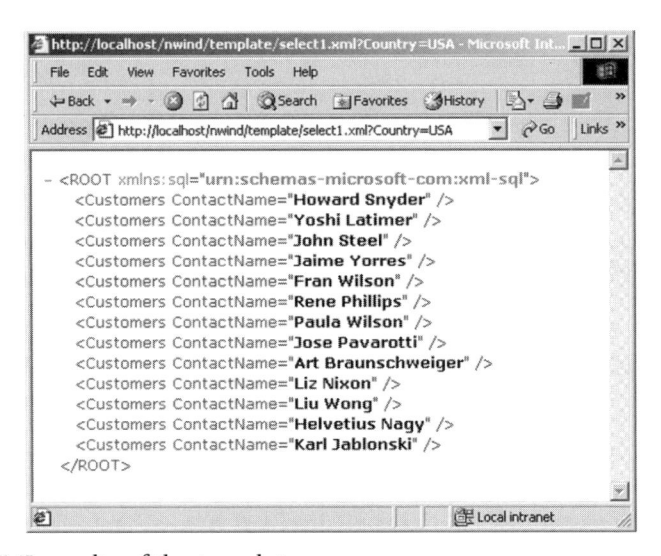

Figure 8-2: XML results of the template query

on the Web server, users cannot alter the query other than by specifying parameter values. Second, you can configure Web server security settings and specify different permissions on individual templates so that you can control access to queries.

As mentioned previously, you can also directly specify templates in a URL much as you can specify SQL queries in a URL. However, if you think SQL queries are tough to enter in the query string of a URL, try specifying an XML document in a URL. This method does not use a file on the Web server and suffers the same security weaknesses as sending SQL queries in a URL.

XPath Queries

XPath, the XML query language introduced in a sidebar in Chapter 7, is an alternative way to query SQL Server databases. XPath queries can be submitted in URLs directly, or they can be specified in template files. However, unlike SQL queries, XPath queries require an additional element called an *XML view*, which I'll talk about shortly.

HTTP Post Queries

In addition to sending queries using a URL, SQL and XPath queries can also be submitted to the server using the HTTP POST method of submission. POST is the method typically used to submit HTML forms to a Web server. In fact, you can submit queries using HTML forms and add input fields that you can provide so users can enter values for parameters to the query. What you submit to the Web server is a template query, either SQL or XPath, and any parameter values required. This method of submission also allows client applications to submit any query they choose, so again you should limit access to this feature or deny access entirely.

XML Views

XML Views are XML representations of part of a database schema created for the purpose of exposing a portion of the database to access by XPath queries. They are defined using the XML Data–Reduced (XDR) language, which is an alternative to DTDs for defining XML document schemas. It is based on the XML Data specification, submitted to the W3C in 1998, which is one of many languages that have been proposed to the W3C as an alternative to DTDs. However, at the time of this writing, the W3C moved ever closer to recommending a different alternative language, called XML Schema, as the "standard" alternative to DTDs. Microsoft helped develop and propose the XML Data language, on which XDR is based. However, Microsoft chose to come to market quickly with a solution that worked today rather than waiting for a standards body to approve a new standard language tomorrow.

> **Note**
>
> Without getting into the history of DTDs and alternatives too deeply, it is important to understand why DTDs are generally not appropriate for defining schemas for XML documents that represent relational schemas. First, relational databases support a rich set of data types. DTDs support only strings and therefore cannot adequately represent the many types of data that can be stored in a database. This one reason alone is enough to think twice before choosing DTDs as the language for specifying XML document structures to represent relational schemas. In addition, DTDs are not written in XML and, therefore, require additional logic to parse and to validate a document against them. Alternative languages like XDR and XML Schema are both based in XML and can be read, parsed, and validated by standard XML parsers. For these and many other reasons, several standards including XDR and XML Schema have been proposed over the last few years as alternatives to DTDs for certain applications.

But XML views are more than just document schemas defined in XDR. XDR schemas simply define the structure of a document. They do not explicitly map elements and attributes in the document to specific database objects, such as tables and columns. XML views require additional information in order to define the mapping between the XDR schema and the relational schema.

Microsoft provides additional attributes for use in annotating XDR schemas with mapping information that describes how the elements in an XDR schema relate to elements in a relational schema. Microsoft refers to these schemas as *annotated XDR schemas*, which is also known as an *XML view*. The annotations are really just XML attributes that can be applied to various elements defined in an XDR schema. For instance, you can add an attribute or annotate an element definition to note that the element represents a table in a database. This kind of annotation may be used to help an application that is reading an XML document based on the annotated schema handle the various elements by knowing more about what those elements represent. For example, some elements may be annotated to indicate that they represent tables in the database. Other elements may be marked as columns. Additional annotations, such as ones marking columns as primary key columns, are also available.

As mentioned earlier, one way to retrieve SQL Server data in XML format across HTTP is to define XML views. You do so by defining annotated XDR schemas, storing those schemas on the Web server, and then passing XPath queries against those XML views. You can send the query through the URL, via HTTP POST or by using a template file. All of the features of XDR provide a way in XDR to define a rich schema for representing relational database elements in your XML views.

By now, you might be asking yourself why in the world you'd want to go to all of this trouble to query a relational database with XPath when you could use good, old SQL instead. The answer to this question is simple. If your application requirements can be satisfied by good, old SQL, then by all means just use SQL. The XML features of SQL Server 2000 aren't intended to be generic alternatives to SQL for retrieving data; they are intended for use in applications that require XML output or that can benefit from using XML and related technologies.

The major reason to use XML views and XPath queries is that it is often simpler to get XML results in a complex format using XML views than it is using SQL queries with the FOR XML EXPLICIT option. FOR XML EXPLICIT gives you a great deal of control over the format of the returned results, but it can be very cumbersome to use. XML views provide a more structured and reusable way to specify the format of your XML results.

Another reason to use XML views and XPath may be to support code reuse. For example, suppose that you already have an application that uses XPath to query a corpus of XML documents. Perhaps as your application grows, you find that you must integrate data from some corporate databases into your results.

Or you might find that you could benefit from partial decomposition by storing some information in a relational database. In such cases, you wouldn't want to rewrite drastically your XPath-based applications to work with a relational database. The alternative is to retrieve some of your data using SQL and some of your data using XPath and trying to marry them in some way. I can tell you from experience that using disparate technologies to retrieve data and attempting to marry them into a unified view is not a pleasant exercise. By defining XML views on your relational data, you can leverage your existing XPath code to query the relational data using the same technologies, and perhaps even some of the same code, as you use to query your XML documents.[1]

Defining XML Views

XDR isn't the most pleasant language to work with when coding by hand. And once you have defined an XDR schema, you're not finished defining your XML view. You still have to annotate it in order to map the XDR schema to the relational schema. In addition, it is possible that XDR may not become an approved W3C standard. While no one can say for sure, Microsoft may drop support for XDR in favor of the XML Schema standard.

To help save you time both learning XDR and applying it, I'm going to show you two things that will help you define XML views more productively with less XDR coding. First, I'll demonstrate a SQL query trick that you can use to generate part or all of an XDR schema automatically. Then I'll show you the XML View Mapper tool that Microsoft built to help developers visually annotate XDR schemas without coding.

There are three steps to defining an XML view:

1. Identify the elements of your database schema that you want to expose in the view.
2. Build an XDR schema that represents the relational schema, including data type information and other properties, such as key columns.
3. Annotate the XDR schema with mapping information.

[1.] At the time of this writing, XPath is the only XML query language supported by SQL Server. For examples of the XPath syntax, see the sidebar XPath in Chapter 7.

Let's dive into an example to show how to define XML views, as well as how to do it productively rather than simply doing everything by hand. Why do everything by hand when tools and tricks that can help us work more efficiently are available? After all, the more efficiently we work, the more time we'll have to catch up on Dilbert.

If you are the type that enjoys the palpable pleasure of hacking out every last character of code, you'll find that annotated XDR schemas are well documented in the SQL Server Books Online documentation.

Let's take a deeper look at the Northwind database that ships with SQL Server. Figure 8-3 shows a partial entity relationship diagram (which alert readers should recognize as a variant of our data model diagrams from Chapter 4) of the database schema representing Customers, Orders, and the relationship between them.

For this example, we'll create an XML view that represents the Orders table. Notice that the Orders table contains a reference to the Customer that placed the order. We'll see shortly how that is represented in an annotated XDR schema.

To keep the example brief and focus on the important aspects, we'll represent only the following fields in the view:

- OrderID
- CustomerID
- OrderDate
- ShipCity
- Freight

Now that we've identified the elements we want to represent, we move on to step two in the process and define an XDR schema that models them. We could do this by hand, and SQL Server Books Online can instruct you in all of the fine details of how to build the most exquisite XDR schemas known to man. Or, we can do it the easy way and finish in five minutes.

If we were building an XDR schema by hand, we would essentially be building an XML document because XDR schemas, unlike their cousins, DTDs, are themselves XML documents. They just happen to represent the structure of

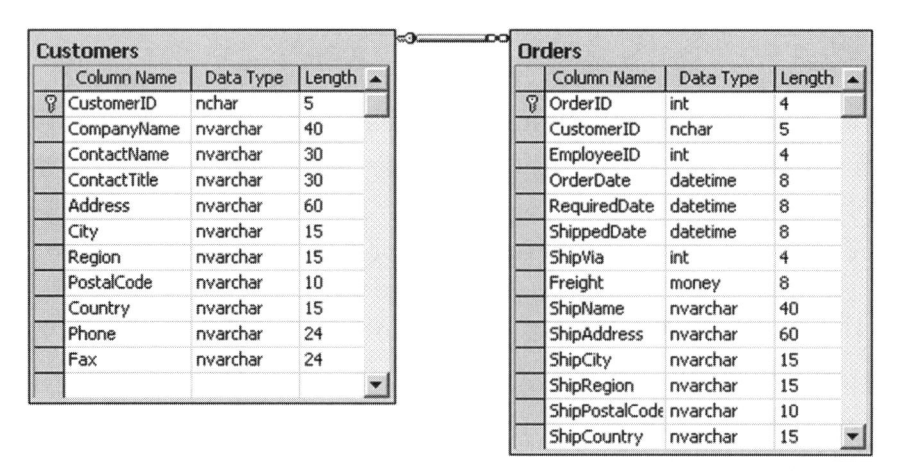

Figure 8-3: Partial representation of the Northwind database schema

other XML documents. However, we're going to save time and use a simple coding trick to define our schema quickly and accurately.

Let SQL Server Do the Work

Our workhorse here is the good, old FOR XML clause, but we're going to use it in an unorthodox, but perfectly legal, fashion. The FOR XML clause takes some optional arguments after the mode argument (RAW, AUTO, or EXPLICIT) discussed earlier in the chapter. You can add the argument XML-DATA after the mode argument, and SQL Server will return some additional information along with your XML data set. This argument tells SQL Server to return not only the result set formatted in XML, but also an XDR schema that defines the structure of XML data returned. How convenient!

Executing a query that returns fields of the tables that you want in your XDR schema is one way to get a good start on building an XDR schema for your XML view. Let's look at how we could use this off-label use of XMLDATA to generate most, if not all, of our XDR schema automatically.

For our example we simply want a few fields from a single table. This query should give us what we need:

```
SELECT OrderID, CustomerID, OrderDate, ShipCity, Freight
FROM Orders
```

```
WHERE OrderID = 0
FOR XML AUTO, XMLDATA
```

In this case, I don't care if any actual rows of data are returned because I'm interested only in the XDR schema that SQL Server will generate. So I've specified a value for the OrderID in the WHERE clause that I know won't return any rows.

SQL Server returns the following results:

```
<Schema name="Schema1" xmlns="urn:schemas-microsoft-com:xml-data"
xmlns:dt="urn:schemas-microsoft-com:datatypes">
   <ElementType name="Orders" content="empty" model="closed">
      <AttributeType name="OrderID" dt:type="i4" />
      <AttributeType name="CustomerID" dt:type="string" />
      <AttributeType name="OrderDate" dt:type="dateTime" />
      <AttributeType name="ShipCity" dt:type="string" />
      <AttributeType name="Freight" dt:type="fixed.14.4" />
      <attribute type="OrderID" />
      <attribute type="CustomerID" />
      <attribute type="OrderDate" />
      <attribute type="ShipCity" />
      <attribute type="Freight" />
   </ElementType>
</Schema>
```

Look at that! By executing a simple query, we're almost done writing the entire XML view, and we wrote only one line of SQL code to do it.

The schema definition is pretty straightforward, but since this is the first time we've looked at an XDR schema, I want to highlight a few aspects. The Orders table is defined as an XML element, and its fields are defined as attributes of that element. This sounds very similar to the way SQL Server formats results when you execute queries using the AUTO mode of the FOR XML clause. The data types of the columns are also defined. The string and dateTime types are straightforward enough. The i4 data type represents a 4-byte integer value. The data type fixed.14.4 represents a decimal value that can have no more than 14 digits to the left of the decimal and 4 digits to the right.

If this query had returned data, we could strip off all of the XML data returned in the query in a simple text editor. We want only the XDR schema. Depending on how we executed the query, the results might not be formatted very well. I executed this query by URL encoding it and sending it in a URL. Internet Explorer returned the results and formatted them nicely. If I had executed the query in the SQL Server Query Analyzer tool, the results would have been returned as a string with no linefeeds or indentation.

We can clean up the formatting in several ways. We can do it by hand, although this method is time-consuming and about as interesting as mowing the lawn by plucking out each blade of grass one by one. Another way is to write a small program or script, using a language such as Visual Basic or JavaScript, that inserts line feeds and white space in certain places to format the document. This method can also be reused when you generate other schemas. Though by far the simplest method I've found is to save the schema to a text file and then open that file in an XML editor, such as XML Spy. Then, simply save the file from the XML editor back into the same file, and the editor rearranges the document into a nice, readable format with line feeds and white space in the appropriate spots. Choose whichever method you feel more comfortable with.

Note

I want to bring to your attention one important note about the XMLDATA argument. Microsoft warns that generating XDR schemas with XMLDATA uses more resources on the server than simply returning data in XML format. So you probably should avoid using it to generate XDR schemas at runtime in your applications. But, when used during development as a way to save time in defining XDR schemas, it works great and shouldn't impact the performance of your server at all.

Now that you have an XDR schema, the third and final step in the process for creating an XML view is to annotate the XDR schema and map the schema to relational database elements. Again, you can do this by hand, or you can do it the easy way. Microsoft provides a tool, called XML View Mapper, that lets you graphically map an XDR schema that has not been annotated to elements in a relational database schema. The output is an annotated version of the XDR schema. At the time of this writing, this tool did not ship with SQL Server 2000, but it was available as a free download from Microsoft's Web site.

Note

You can find XML View Mapper on Microsoft's MSDN Web site at http://msdn.microsoft.com/

As you can see, the SQL Server XML View Mapper is a helpful little tool. It's also multifunctional. Not only can it help you define your annotated XDR schemas, but it also has utilities you can use to derive an XDR schema from an XML document, convert a DTD to an XDR schema, and do a few other useful functions. Figure 8-4 shows a screen shot of the XML View Mapper at work mapping the Orders table in the Northwind database to the XDR schema that was generated previously.

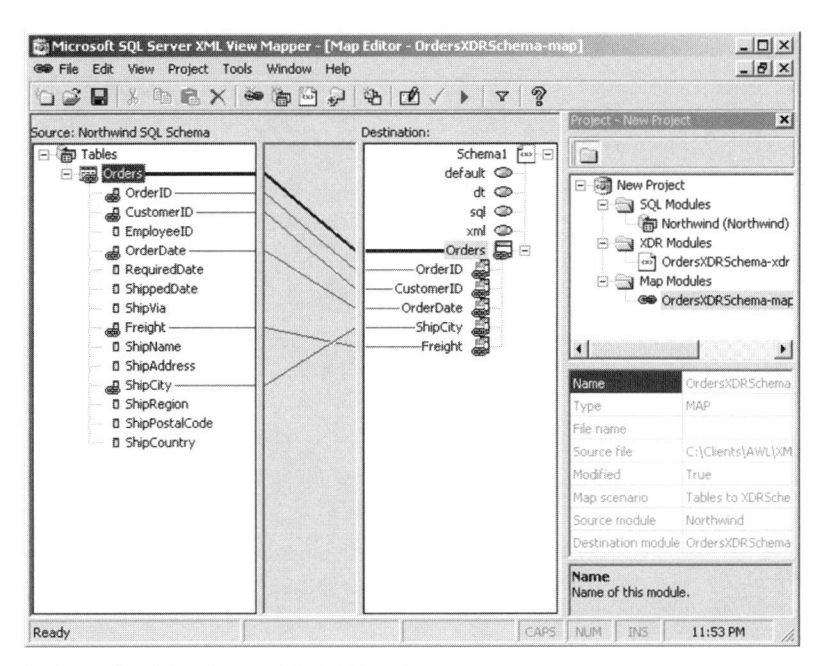

Figure 8-4: The SQL Server XML View Mapper

After I'm finished mapping, I can save the result to a text file and generate the annotated XDR schema.

```xml
<?xml   version="1.0" ?>
<!-- Generated by XMLMapper.exe XDR Publisher -->
<Schema name="Schema1"
        xmlns="urn:schemas-microsoft-com:xml-data"
        xmlns:dt="urn:schemas-microsoft-com:datatypes"
        xmlns:sql="urn:schemas-microsoft-com:xml-sql" >
 <ElementType name="Orders"
              model="closed"
              content="empty"
              order="many" >
   <AttributeType name="OrderID"
                  dt:type="i4" >
   </AttributeType>
   <AttributeType name="CustomerID"
                  dt:type="string" >
   </AttributeType>
   <AttributeType name="OrderDate"
                  dt:type="dateTime" >
   </AttributeType>
   <AttributeType name="ShipCity"
                  dt:type="string" >
   </AttributeType>
   <AttributeType name="Freight"
                  dt:type="fixed.14.4" >
   </AttributeType>
   <attribute type="OrderID"
              required="no" >
   </attribute>
   <attribute type="CustomerID"
              required="no" >
   </attribute>
   <attribute type="OrderDate"
```

```
                required="no" >
    </attribute>
    <attribute type="ShipCity"
                required="no" >
    </attribute>
    <attribute type="Freight"
                required="no" >
    </attribute>
 </ElementType>
</Schema>
```

Aside from the slightly different format of the document, there aren't too many changes from the original XDR Schema. The first significant change is the addition of an attribute of order with a value of many to the ElementType definition of the Orders element type. The order attribute defines in what order the elements of this element type may appear in a document based on this schema. A value of many indicates that the elements can occur in any order. Also notice that each of the attributes has a value of no for the require attributes. This means that these attributes do not have to be specified for any given Order element. However, this value has also been set for the OrderID column. I don't want this value to be optional, nor do I want the CustomerID value to be optional, so I'll change them to be required.

```
    <attribute type="OrderID"
                required="yes" >
    </attribute>
    <attribute type="CustomerID"
                required="yes" >
    </attribute>
```

While the process of defining XDR Schemas and mapping them to a relational database using the XML View Mapper tool is straightforward, it is still somewhat clunky. I hope that in the future Microsoft will make the process of mapping database schemas to XML documents an even simpler, more integrated process.

Working with XML Documents

I've shown you how to turn relational data into XML data; now let's look at how you can turn XML data into relational data. SQL Server provides features for working with XML documents on the server and even for writing data from XML documents to the database. The OPENXML keyword and two system-stored procedures that I'll discuss provide a way to access XML documents within queries as if they were a standard relational table. However, as you'll discover, the syntax for accessing portions of an XML document is specialized.

OPENXML

Here's a simple example of how OPENXML is typically used. The example simply demonstrates how to query an XML document using a SQL SELECT query.

```
DECLARE @hdlXmlDoc integer
DECLARE @xmlText varchar(2000)

SET @xmlText = '<?xml  version="1.0" ?>
<RESULTS>
   <Orders OrderID="10643" CustomerID="ALFKI" Freight="29.46" />
   <Orders OrderID="10692" CustomerID="ALFKI" Freight="61.02" />
   <Orders OrderID="10702" CustomerID="ALFKI" Freight="23.94" />
   <Orders OrderID="10835" CustomerID="ALFKI" Freight="69.53" />
   <Orders OrderID="10952" CustomerID="ALFKI" Freight="40.42" />
   <Orders OrderID="11011" CustomerID="ALFKI" Freight="1.21" />
</RESULTS>'

exec sp_xml_preparedocument @hdlXmlDoc OUTPUT, @xmlText

SELECT OrderID, Freight
FROM OPENXML (@hdlXmlDoc, '/RESULTS/Orders', 1)
   WITH (OrderID integer,
        Freight real)
WHERE Freight = 1.21

exec sp_xml_removedocument @hdlXmlDoc
```

Dissecting the code, we can see one big potential problem. We're not operating on an XML document in a file, but rather the text is just stored in a string variable. This doesn't seem practical because most of the XML text anyone wants to work with resides in text files. You can eliminate this limitation by wrapping your queries that rely on OPENXML in stored procedures and by passing in the XML text from a document as a parameter to the stored procedure. This does require that the calling application, such as a Visual Basic or Java application, first open the XML text file and extract the text. The calling application then calls the stored procedure and passes the text in as a parameter value.

```
CREATE PROCEDURE spGetOrder
(
    @xmlText varchar(2000),
    @orderID integer
)
AS

DECLARE    @hdlXmlDoc integer

exec sp_xml_preparedocument @hdlXmlDoc OUTPUT, @xmlText

SELECT OrderID, Freight
FROM OPENXML (@hdlXmlDoc, '/RESULTS/Orders', 1)
    WITH (OrderID integer,
          Freight real)
WHERE Freight = 1.21

exec sp_xml_removedocument @hdlXmlDoc

GO
```

Continuing with our examination of the OPENXML statement, notice that it is being used in the FROM clause of the SQL query as if it were a table. You've probably also noticed that I'm calling two system-stored procedures, sp_xml_preparedocument and sp_xml_removedocument. The first procedure, sp_xml_preparedocument, opens the XML document and prepares it for reading. SQL Server actually reads the entire document structure into memory and holds it there, much as any XML DOM parser would do. In fact, SQL Server is actually using a DOM parser (the Microsoft MSXML parser, to be exact) to parse the XML document.

Once I'm finished using the document, I call the counterpart, sp_xml_removedocument, to close the XML document and free system resources used to hold it in memory. Because SQL Server pulls the entire file into memory upon calling sp_xml_preparedocument and keeps it there in parsed form until you call the cleanup stored procedure, you should avoid opening very large XML files in this manner. And always call the cleanup stored procedure as soon as you are done with the file to free memory as soon as possible.

> **Note**
>
> It is possible to read XML instances efficiently into SQL Server. SQL Server provides an XML bulk copy feature that does not use a DOM parser and does not load the entire document into memory. Instead, its parser handles portions of the document as they are read in and does not need to keep the entire document in memory in order to work with it.

The final important aspect of the example that you should take note of is the use of XPath to tell SQL Server exactly which portion of the XML document should be represented as a table by the OPENXML keyword. The XPath query selects all of the Orders elements—all rows and attributes—in the document. The WITH statement defines the attributes we want to extract, which will become columns in the SQL result set and the SQL data types of the columns.

The example showed only how to select data from an XML document. You can also use OPENXML in the context of INSERT, UPDATE, and DELETE statements as well. This means you can extract data from XML documents and insert it into a database or update relational data. In the context of a DELETE statement, you can use the set of data provided by OPENXML, such as a list of primary key values, to determine which records in your relational database to delete.

Summary

In this chapter, I discussed the features of Microsoft SQL Server 2000 that enable you to work with XML and relate XML documents and SQL Server database objects. I showed you several ways to retrieve data, including the FOR XML clause, templates, XML views, and XPath queries.

You learned how to communicate with SQL Server across the HTTP protocol by formatting your requests, using various methods, in XML. I also discussed some tips and tricks that should make building XML views simpler than writing them entirely by hand.

Finally, the OPENXML feature enables you to open XML documents on SQL Server so you can query and insert data into your databases directly from the XML documents. Still more features are available with SQL Server. I recommend that you explore them if you find that implementing XML processing on your database server is appropriate for the requirements of your projects.

While this chapter has illustrated some of the mechanics of how one vendor has married XML and SQL databases, other major database vendors, such as Oracle, also offer features for integrating XML and relational databases. With this knowledge in hand, you should be well prepared to begin exploring the features of your favorite server in greater depth for whatever applications you choose to build.

Chapter 9

Java Programming with XML and SQL

> In which the TLAs come out in full force.

So far in this book, we've looked at XML and relational databases and some strategies for combining the two to create powerful applications. In Chapter 8, we looked at ways to build specific database structures in a real-world database. In this chapter, I discuss building your application code in Java with a J2EE-type application server.

Produced by Sun, the J2EE (Java 2 Enterprise Edition) specification gives application server vendors a baseline for how their software should behave in order to be J2EE-compliant. This means that a J2EE application should work in any J2EE-compliant application server.

I'm a big fan of server-side Java. which I've been using since 1996. At that time, most people looked at you funny when you said "server side Java." Java was thought of as a language for building funny little animations on Web pages. That was one way Sun was marketing it, but I saw in Java an opportunity to build on the server side simple Web applications that would be a perfect replacement for all the crusty Perl scripts we had been writing in the small Web consulting business I was involved with. Why? Java is an object-oriented language; it is simple to use and to get started in (especially compared with C++), and it comes with built-in APIs to support functions (such as HTTP requests, string parsing, URL management, and database connections) often needed when building Web applications. Today, the J2EE standard, which evolved from those humble beginnings in 1996, is one of the most widely used application environments for Web applications, and most people have forgotten about the Web page animations that started it all.

The J2EE specification basically consists of Enterprise Java Beans (EJBs—self-contained objects that conform to a specific standard) that interact with back-end data sources, servlets (the server equivalent of a Java applet—a Java program that runs on the server side and responds to HTTP requests, possibly calling out to functionality in deeper level EJBs in the process), and Java Server Pages, abbreviated JSP, (which essentially are a specialized form of servlet and Sun's answer to Microsoft's Active Server Pages) on the front end that interact with client programs over HTTP.

The rest of the J2EE specification consists of a set of class libraries that allow these servlets and EJBs to perform specific functions (such as the Java DataBase Connectivity layer—JDBC—that allows for connection to back-end data sources or the JavaMail API that provides functions for dealing with e-mail messages programmatically). The idea is that the business logic of your application should exist in the EJBs and all client interaction should happen at the servlet layer. A basic diagram of how these layers interact is shown in Figure 9-1.

You could write an entire book on Java and XML, but someone already has: *XML and Java: Developing Web Applications* by Hiroshi Maruyama, Kent Tamura, and Naohiko Uramoto (1999). This chapter provides an overview of some of the features of the J2EE framework and the JAXP (Java API for XML Processing) that apply mostly to building applications with XML and SQL.

Much of the material presented in this chapter will make the most sense to a developer who's already familiar with the Java language—this isn't a primer on Java. If you're not planning to use Java, I suggest you at least read the following sidebar on the SAX and DOM parsers (Parsers: SAX versus DOM). You may want to read through the brief examples on using SAX and DOM as well. For those of you planning on developing with Java, this chapter will be more relevant.

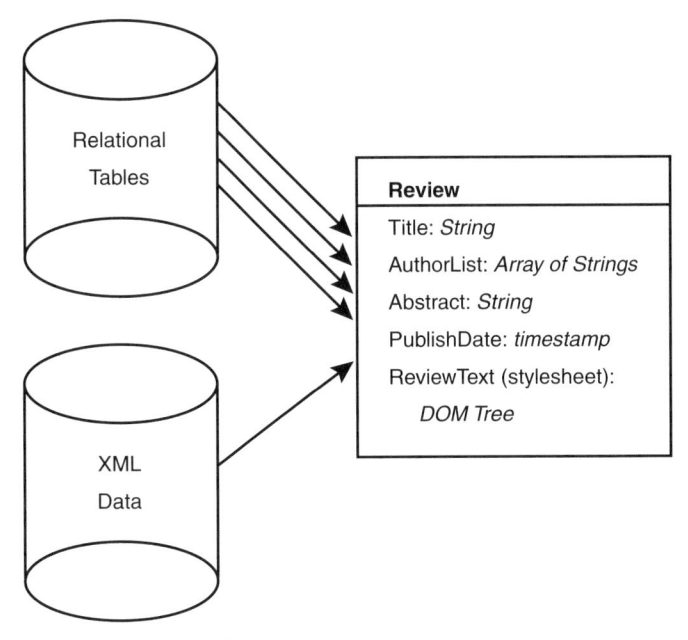

Figure 9-1: The J2EE application framework

Dealing with XML in Java

JAXP (Java API for XML Processing) is a standard set of Java APIs for dealing with XML objects. It's not strictly part of the J2EE standard, but it's an essential class library for dealing with XML instances. JDBC (Java DataBase Connectivity) is a set of Java APIs for connecting to back-end SQL databases. Together, JAXP and JDBC provide an infrastructure for building applications using XML and SQL. One way JAXP and JDBC work together is in the construction of Java objects that utilize both APIs to provide seamless access to information encoded in both XML and relational databases.

Parsers: SAX Versus DOM

As if you needed more impenetrable acronyms in your life!

Whenever you deal with XML instances in applications (Java or otherwise), you need to think about XML parsers. An XML parser turns the raw XML document into something that your application can use. SAX (Simple API for XML) and DOM (Document Object Model) are two different approaches that are used across different programming languages and application servers. Both take XML instances and turn them into something that can be manipulated programmatically, but they take very different paths to get there.

SAX (http://www.megginson.com/SAX/) uses an "event-based" model, which means that, as a SAX parser processes through your XML instance, it kicks off events that your code can "listen" for. Anyone who's written user interface code should be familiar with event-based coding. Your code listens for an event (such as a mouse click or a key press) and then kicks off some functionality based on this event. In the case of SAX events, you're waiting for a certain tag or combination of tags.

DOM takes a different, and somewhat more involved, approach, converting your entire XML instance into a tree and handing it back to you in that form. It's then up to you to walk through that tree from node to node, or search through it for what you're looking for.

The bottom line is that SAX is lighter weight, but DOM is much more powerful. With SAX, you create an object model for your data and map SAX-parsed XML into your object model. One advantage of SAX is that your application's object model can be exactly what you want it to be. DOM creates an object model for you. Choosing whether to use SAX or DOM depends on what kind of data is in your XML and how you want to use it. If you're doing something simple with XML messages being passed back and forth between systems, the lighter-weight SAX is your best bet. If you're doing anything more complex (for example, working with documents like our example movie reviews or complex hierarchical data) or if you are writing a user-oriented application that manipulates XML instances, you should use DOM. If you're building routines to do partial decomposition, I recommend using SAX because the event-based model makes more sense in this context. SAX is the parser to use if you want to manipulate XML documents "on the fly" or where storage capacity is limited (such as in a mobile device) because it doesn't require huge amounts of memory to store a document tree as DOM does.

Both SAX and DOM parsers are included in the JAXP specification, and by the way, nothing stops you from using both in the same application.

DOM (http://www.w3.org/DOM/) was developed by the W3C. DOM Level 2 has recently been released as a recommended specification. DOM Level 2 allows for an XML event model (bringing it closer to SAX in terms of functionality) and includes some other useful features. Many commercial XML parsers currently on the market support DOM Level 2.

Building Java Objects for XML Instances with DOM

In many cases, especially when your application code has to work with many of your documents simultaneously, you need to create an object type for your document instances. For the kind of XML instances we've been dealing with in this book and when you already have relational tables that contain data partially decomposed from the XML, I recommend building custom objects around a DOM-parsed tree and information retrieved directly from the relational tables. As the Review object (a simplified version of our movie review examples from the previous chapters) in Figure 9-2 illustrates, the title, author list, abstract, and publish date are represented by simple Java types—strings, arrays of strings, and timestamps (the latter being a JDBC type but still simple). These pieces of information are extracted directly from relational tables of the kind that we discussed in Chapter 6. The review text itself is stored in a DOM tree, which is parsed from the XML instance itself—probably, but not necessarily, from the same database.

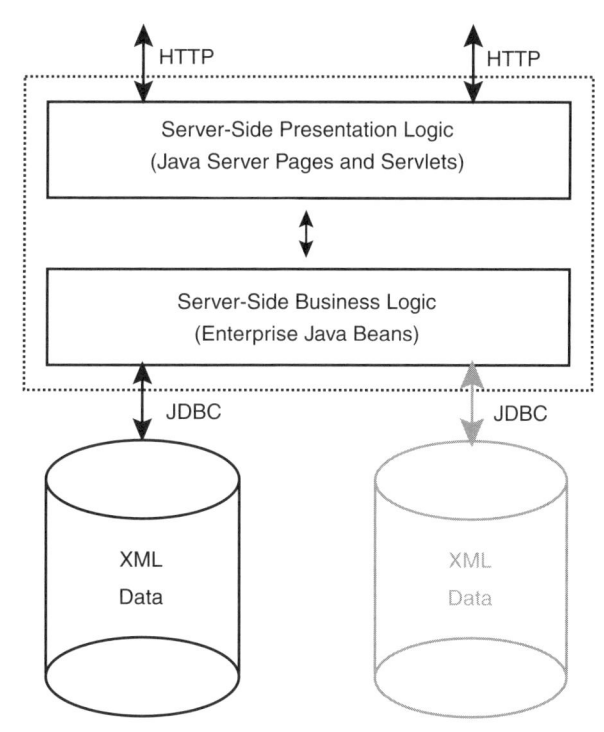

Figure 9-2: Review object with data sources

Your review object, when instantiated, should populate its simple fields (such as Title, Author, Abstract, and Publish Date) but wait to populate the ReviewText field until this data is asked for. In this manner, you save yourself the trouble of parsing the XML document and storing the tree in memory until it's needed. Your application may have instantiated this object only as part of an array of reviews so that it can display a listing of reviews, showing the title, author, abstract, and publish date. The user, using your application, then selects one of the reviews for reading, at which point you can go back to the database, extract the XML instance, and parse it using a DOM parser to create the tree object necessary for whatever action you wish. Or you can send it to an XSLT transformation as described later (see the section Invoking XSLT Transformations later in this chapter).

The code you execute to build your DOM tree when needed would look something like this:

```
static Document myDocument;
DocumentBuilderFactory factory =
    DocumentBuilderFactory.newInstance();
...
try {
    DocumentBuilder builder = factory.newDocumentBuilder();
    myDocument = builder.parse( ...the source of the XML instance... );

} catch (Exception x) {
// Do something with any exceptions generated
}
```

In this example, I've used the DocumentBuilderFactory class, which is part of the JAXP library (under the class hierarchy javax.xml.parsers) to give me a DocumentBuilder object whenever I need one. This approach simplifies your code by relying on an object factory to create your DocumentBuilder objects for you instead of having to instantiate and initialize them yourself. This DocumentBuilder object is then used to parse the XML file (probably taken out of the database using JDBC; it returns a parsed DOM tree into myDocument.

Using SAX Events to Drive XML Partial Decomposition

A SAX parser generates specific events as it processes through an XML instance. The generic `DefaultHandler` class (which is actually defined in the `org.xml.sax.helpers` package that provides many other useful helper classes and utility functions) is provided for you to subclass and add your own functionality to. The main event-handling methods provided (as null methods) are `startDocument` (which triggers at the start of an XML instance), `endDocument` (which triggers at the end of an XML instance), `startElement` (which triggers at the beginning of an element), `endElement` (which triggers at the end of an element), and `characters` (which handles all characters contained with in elements, including white space). When the parser is invoked on an XML instance, the parser throws Java exceptions that correspond to these events. Those exceptions can then be caught by whatever code invoked the parser to begin with.

When the parser finds a start tag or end tag, the name of the tag is passed to the `startElement` or `endElement` method. When a start tag is encountered, its attributes are passed as a list. Characters found in the element are also passed along.

The upshot of all this is that your custom-coded methods can wait for the SAX events described earlier and then execute JDBC statements to insert or update information in your relational tables or call preprepared, stored SQL procedures within your relational database. Your resultant code would look something like this:

```
import org.xml.sax.*;
import javax.xml.parsers.SAXParserFactory;
import javax.xml.parsers.ParserConfigurationException;
import javax.xml.parsers.SAXParser;

public class MyFunXMLHandler extends DefaultHandler
{
    public void startDocument()
    throws SAXException
    {
```

```
        // Whatever you want to do at the start of the document -- maybe
        // open your connection to the database.
    }

    public void endDocument()
    throws SAXException
    {
        // Whatever you want to do at the end of the document -- maybe close
        // your connection to the database.
    }

    public void startElement(String namespaceURI,  // Only used if we're using
                             String localName,      // using XML name spaces…
                             String qualifiedName,
                             Attributes attributes)
    throws SAXException
    {
    // Call a partial decomposition utility function with the name of
    // the element and attribute list as parameters.
    }

}
```

This code skeleton shows how you can set up the parser to process through code and react to SAX parser events. The first part imports the necessary class libraries. You don't need to override the default method for `endElement` because you don't need to do anything special when an element ends.

The `namespaceURI` and `localName` parameters to startElement are used only if you're using XML namespaces, which is a method for creating a standard reference for the names of elements and attributes across different applications, schemas, and DTDs. XML namespaces is a fascinating topic, but it is beyond the scope of this book; refer to the W3C recommendation document at http://www.w3.org/TR/1999/REC-xml-names-19990114/.

Harkening back to our CyberCinema example, if you're trying to decompose the following piece of XML code:

```
<DOCUMENT ID="23">
…
<MOVIE ID="12">Ben Hur</MOVIE>
…
</DOCUMENT>
```

with the preceding SAX parser, your helper utility will want to insert a row into your `review_movie` bridging table (see Chapter 6), so the corresponding JDBC call will look something like this:

```
String updateString = "INSERT review_movie " +
                      "values (" +
                      reviewId +
                      "," +
                      movieId +
                      ")";
Statement stmt = con.createStatement();
stmt.executeUpdate(updateString);
```

`reviewId` has been set to 23, and `movieId` has been set to 12.

The preceding code works great if the only information you ever want to decompose from the database is stored in element attributes. If you want to decompose the contents of elements, you have to use the `endElement` method and the `characters` method to extract all the information between the beginning of the tag and the end of the tag for decomposition.

Invoking XSLT Transformations

So what do you do when you actually want to *look* at some of this XML? As we saw in Chapter 7, XSLT (Extensible Stylesheet Language Transformation) provides a mechanism for transforming (or converting) one type of XML into another. Your XML servlets (which serve HTTP requests) use XSLT stylesheets to transform the XML code you're using in your application to whatever is appropriate for the particular content delivery channel (another custom XML format, XHTML, WML, and so on). JAXP provides an easy way to convert your

XML instances using XSLT transformations. The following code example illustrates how to invoke XSLT stylesheets from within your Java code:

```
Transformer transformer;
TransformerFactory factory = TransformerFactory.newInstance();
String stylesheet = "file:///cybercinema_root/cc_stylesheet.xsl";
String sourceId = "file:///cybercinema_root/reviews/1234.xml";
try {
  transformer = factory.newTransformer(
      new StreamSource(stylesheet)
      );
  transformer.transform(
      new StreamSource(sourceId),
      new StreamResult(System.out)
      );
} catch (Exception e) {
  // handle whatever exceptions occur
}
```

This code snippet takes a style sheet from one file and an XML instance from another file and outputs the result (the fully transformed file) to the console. You can use this same method to take your XML file from any location (the database, an object in memory, a Web service, anywhere) and transform it. The preceding example is purposely simplistic, but you can begin to see how easily this kind of function is implemented.

Designing an Entity Bean for Movie Reviews

The following code is a simplified design for an entity EJB (Enterprise Java Bean) for our movie reviews. The J2EE spec contains two types of EJBs: session beans and entity beans. Session beans are intended for business processes, while entity beans are intended for business objects (code objects that represent some kind of real-world object, such as an e-mail message, a movie review, a person, an airplane, and so on). For instance, the hypothetical publishing system for our movie reviews might contain session beans that take care of publishing activity (such as maintaining workflow states—see Chapter

10 for a discussion on workflow) and entity beans that represent particular movie reviews.

The code presented here is a first try at entity beans for movie reviews. In this case, I've simplified the reviews by having them include only a review author (pulled directly out of a relational table) and the review XML itself (also pulled out of a table and then parsed into a DOM tree). Note how the database routine `selectByReviewId` first selects the author ID out of the review_person table (which we defined in Chapter 6), then selects the appropriate XML out of the `review` table, and finally parses it using the DOM parser into a `Document` object.

```
// Import required class libraries
//
import java.sql.*;
import javax.sql.*;
import java.util.*;
import javax.ejb.*;
import javax.naming.*;
import javax.xml.parsers.DocumentBuilder;
import javax.xml.parsers.DocumentBuilderFactory;
import org.w3c.dom.Document;


// Define our MovieReview entity bean and all its methods
//
public class MovieReview implements EntityBean
{
    private String reviewId;
    private String authorId;
    private Document document;
    private EntityContext context;
    private Connection con; // database connection
    private String logicalDBName = "...URI for data source...";

    // Public get method for the review ID
    //
    public String getReviewId()
```

```
{
  return reviewId;
}

// Public get method for the review Author
//
public int getAuthorId()
{
   return authorId;
}

// Public get method for the review XML tree
//
public int getDocument()
{
   return document;
}

// Find method for this bean.
//
public String ejbFindByReviewId(String reviewId)
  throws FinderException
{

  String reviewId;

  try
    {
       reviewId = selectByReviewId(reviewId);
     }
  catch (Exception ex)
     {
       throw new EJBException("ejbFindByReviewId: " +
                       ex.getMessage());
     }

  return reviewId;
```

```java
}

// Database routine: initiate connection to database
//
private void makeConnection() throws NamingException, SQLException
{
  InitialContext ic = new InitialContext();
  DataSource ds = (DataSource) ic.lookup(logicalDBName);
  con =  ds.getConnection();
}


// Database routine: get the review author, and get and parse the review
// XML instance.
//
private String selectByReviewId(String reviewId)
  throws SQLException
{
String reviewId;
String reviewXML;
int REVIEWER_ROLE_ID = 3; // This constant for the ID number of the
                          // reviewer role in the review_person_role
                          // table would normally be set
                          // somewhere else, but is here for simplicity.

// Execute the SQL statement to get the review
//
String selectStatement =
        "select person_id, review_xml" +
        "from review, review_person_role" +
        "where review.review_id = ? and review_person_role.role_id = ?";
PreparedStatement prepStmt =
        con.prepareStatement(selectStatement);
prepStmt.setString(1, reviewId);
prepStmt.setString(2, REVIEWER_ROLE_ID);

ResultSet rs = prepStmt.executeQuery();
```

```
    // Extract the author ID and the XML from the result set
    //
    if (rs.next())
       {
           authorId = rs.getString(1);
           reviewXML = rs.getString(1);
       }
    else
       {
           reviewId = null;
       }

    prepStmt.close();

    // Now create a DOM tree out of the XML
    //
       DocumentBuilderFactory factory =
             DocumentBuilderFactory.newInstance();

       try
       {
          DocumentBuilder builder = factory.newDocumentBuilder();
          document = builder.parse(reviewXML);
       }
    catch (Exception x)
       {
           reviewId= null;;
       }

    return reviewId;
    }
}
```

Now we have a way to create for our movie reviews self-contained entity bean objects that can be manipulated by session beans, enumerated, queried, and otherwise shuffled around in the business logic of our application.

To Transform or Not to Transform

The JAXP libraries provide a powerful XML transformation mechanism for XML through invoking XMLT transformations, as we've seen previously in this chapter. However, I don't recommend that you do XML transformation on the fly in your applications. What do I mean by that? Let's take the following example, again building on our CyberCinema example.

When a review is published, it goes through a workflow process and ends up in a database table as a raw bit of XML with some accompanying, partially decomposed data (the author, title, publish date, and so forth) in other tables. Every time a user asks to see this review, do you want to fumble around in your database, pulling out the data, starting up the parser, running the document through the parser, transforming it to HTML, and serving it to the user? The alternative is to invoke the three most important parts of any Web application: *caching, caching, caching.*

Partial decomposition already represents a layer of caching. Some application servers include caching functionality at the database level and at the page generation level, which can be a good start, although I don't necessarily recommend relying on these built-in caching mechanisms. When you design your application, you should think about caching at each layer of your application. If a particular product offers built-in caching that fits the bill for one or more of these layers, then by all means make use of it.

Using the example of page generation, you can take one of several approaches:

- **Pregenerate all pages.** Your document management system can pregenerate the pages that it knows need to be generated whenever a "publishing" action takes place and output them to HTML files sitting in a document root of your Web server. This strategy is the most meticulous type of page management, but when you're talking performance, there is nothing better than serving flat HTML documents off a file system. Don't let the tools vendors tell you differently. The tricky parts are making sure the right HTML documents are regenerated when you need them to be and maintaining "link integrity"—that is, making sure that intradocument links point where they're supposed to and don't point to documents that haven't been generated yet.

- **Use a page-caching application server.** Some application servers include page caches, which generate a requested page on first request and then keep it in a file system cache. Subsequent requests for the same page are served directly out of the file system. The advantage is that you don't have to maintain the set of HTML files yourself, as with the previously described approach. A disadvantage is that these page-caching systems are often somewhat of a "black box" to the developer; that is, when they work, they're great, but when they fail, you have no idea why they've failed and no way to fix them. In addition, page-caching application servers are often prohibitively expensive.
- **Use a reverse-proxy cache in front of your application server.** Another approach that gets you the same bang for fewer bucks is to use a reverse-proxy cache in front of your application server. Squid (http://www.squid-cache.org/) is an excellent free solution for reverse-proxy page caching. The reverse-proxy cache basically responds to all page requests from the Internet—that is, it becomes your Web server, the one users hit when they go to your site. But the reverse-proxy cache has a secret: It isn't really your Web server at all, but it knows where your server is. So if the reverse-proxy cache doesn't have the document the user is looking for, it gets it from the Web server and caches it for a configurable period of time.

The disadvantage of using a page cache that isn't part of your application server is that you don't have fine control over it from your application. Your application can't easily tell it to "forget" a page, which can mean a delay in the publishing process as you wait for your page cache to "flush."

JDBC, JNDI, and EJBs

It seems like JDBC (Java DataBase Connectivity API) has been with us since the dawn of time. It's the reliable old guy who's sitting in the corner smoking his cigar that nobody thinks about any more. But it wasn't always this way. I clearly remember wrestling with so-called "standard" features of JDBC back in 1997. Even getting the JDBC driver to connect to the database was a delicate balancing act and still can be. But assuming your JDBC driver is properly configured, you can be reasonably assured that your Java code can get stuff out of your database and put stuff back in.

JDBC 2.0 went one step beyond the previous version of JDBC in a number of ways, most notably by allowing advanced data types and access to databases through the new Java Naming and Directory Interface (JNDI).

JNDI

Another four-letter acronym beginning with J, and it won't be the last. I wonder why these guys can't come up with more *creative* names for their specifications, like *Viper* or *Crucible*?

Anyway, JNDI, despite its prosaic moniker, is actually exciting because it abstracts the part of your application that requests and instantiates the actual JDBC connection. When you're building J2EE applications, your building blocks are EJBs. These EJBs sit inside containers that are implemented by whatever application server your EJBs are executing in. EJB containers implement an abstraction layer, called the Environment Naming Context (ENC), so that your beans can happily go about their business (encapsulating business logic or representing specific real-world objects) without having to worry about questions like "What kind of JDBC driver am I supposed to be using, and where do I get it?" Your EJB can use JNDI to ask the ENC for a connection to the JDBC data source hooked up to your J2EE application server (there *will* be a quiz on this later) by implementing a method like the following:

```
private Connection getConnection()
       throws SQLException {

   InitialContext jndiContext = new InitialContext();
   DataSource source = (DataSource)
          jndiContext.lookup("java:comp/env/jdbc/myDatabase");
   return source.getConnection();
}
```

In this example, we're looking up the connection to a database and returning that connection. The difference with JNDI is that you can ask the application context for the connection, and it'll return the most appropriate connection as set up in that context. This means that *your* code doesn't have to worry about it; it can all be configured within the application server. With straight JDBC, you have to specify the driver and a hard-coded URI to a particular database, so what JNDI gives you is code portability for the code modules that you write.

Bean Persistence

The amount of work this abstraction layer can do for you depends on what your application server supports. For instance, some application servers support container-managed persistence of EJBs, which means that you never write a line of JDBC code. The EJB container manages all your database activity for you. Call me old-fashioned, but this level of abstraction makes me a little squeamish, especially when I start to think about performance tuning.

With bean-managed persistence, the EJB code you write manages synchronizing its state with the database as directed by the container. You can use JDBC to read from and write to the database, but the EJB container tells your bean when to do each synchronization operation. Bean-managed persistence gives you more flexibility and makes more sense when you're talking about building beans that access partially decomposed XML.

The example entity EJB presented previously uses bean-managed persistence. In that example, the bean populated some fields by simply performing a SQL select through JDBC to get the title of the document from one of the partial decomposition tables. However, the get method for the body might first extract the whole XML instance, then parse it, and finally return the result of a XSLT transformation. In order to implement the example described previously (in the section Building Java Objects for XML Instances with DOM), you need to use bean-managed persistence.

JDBC Advanced Data Types

Advanced data types mean that JDBC now supports all the kinds of data types defined in the SQL:1999 specification. Most notable among these data types are the CLOB (Character Large OBject) and BLOB (Binary Large Object) types, the array type, and more structured types. CLOBs are important because the CLOB type is *perfect* for storing large XML documents. If you don't know how big your XML documents are going to get, then use CLOB data types. Using Arrays and Structs can help you take care of sophisticated logic inside the database (assuming you have a database that can support it). For instance, you can request a movie review from your database and have it return a Struct, which can encapsulate the XML document itself, the title, the abstract, the author, and an array of the links contained in the text (all extracted via individual selects from partially decomposed data in SQL tables). Then you could hold that in memory and parse the XML document, only if it's actually needed.

The benefit of advanced data types is efficiency: The alternative is to make several selects from your application to the database so what JDBC advanced data types give you is a layer of abstraction that simplifies how your application interacts with the database.

On the Near Horizon: XML Data Binding

An interesting up-and-coming specification, still being worked on at this writing, is XML data binding. The idea is to be able to suck in an XML Schema and automatically generate a set of Java classes to deal with XML data of that format. This specification and framework promises to provide an *abstraction layer* on top of your XML data. If you plan on building a Java framework for managing your XML documents, you should take a serious look at XML data binding.

For more up-to-date information on using XML in Java (and specifically within the J2EE framework), go to JavaSoft's page on XML at http://java.sun.com/xml/.

J2EE Application Servers

If you're starting to develop applications in the J2EE framework, you should first and foremost download the J2EE SDK from JavaSoft (http://java.sun.com/j2ee/download.html). That'll get you started in the world of J2EE programming by supplying the basic software development toolkit, including the compiler and standard class libraries. When you actually want to give your creations life, you'll need a proper J2EE server. Here are some links to help you find the Java application server that meets your needs:

- **Allaire JRun at http://www.allaire.com/products/jrun/.** Allaire enables you to download a fully functional version of their J2EE-compliant server from their Web site, for developer use only.
- **ATG Dynamo at http://www.atg.com.** Art Technology Group claims its Dynamo product is fully J2EE-compliant as of version 5. The ATG folks get special mention because they actually invented the concept of the Java Server Page and licensed it back to Sun. A demo version with a limited license is available for download.
- **BEA WebLogic at http://www.bea.com.** BEA's WebLogic product, also available as a download for free trial, is probably the industry's leading application server.
- **The Jakarta Project at http://jakarta.apache.org.** The folks who gave us Apache have undertaken creating their own open-source Java-based application server, built on top of their already existing Tomcat product, which implements JSPs (Java Server Pages) and servlets—two key pieces of the J2EE framework.
- **IBM's Websphere.** IBM doesn't claim that their WebSphere is J2EE-compliant, but that seems largely a matter of marketing; perhaps they don't want to pay the exorbitant licensing fees that Sun charges for the use of the J2EE name. Visit IBM's home page at http://www.ibm.com; then search for WebSphere.

Summary

In this chapter, I've outlined some of the technologies in the J2EE spec that can be most useful when you're building an application with XML and Java. I also want to provide some resources that will be helpful with this effort.

A great online resource for more information is Sun's Java site itself (http://java.sun.com), from which all the software development toolkits and documentation are downloadable. You'll also find easy-to-understand tutorials there. JavaWorld (http://www.javaworld.com) provides developer resources, tutorials, and plenty of best practices information, as well as updates on what's going on in the Java community. O'Reilly's "OnJava" site (http://www.onjava.com) provides an excellent resource for developers with plenty of reference information and advanced topics material. The site includes an entire section devoted to Java and XML with lots of detailed information.

In addition to the topics discussed in this chapter, an enormous number of open-source projects and other projects supported by the Java community in the field of integrating XML and Java are out of the scope of this book. In Chapter 5, I advised you to look at the publicly available DTDs in various Internet repositories to find one that meets your needs; the same goes for Java libraries. Don't reinvent the wheel if a project that has been working toward similar design goals is already out there. OnJava and JavaWorld are both good places to look for these types of projects, but also look to SourceForge (www.sourceforge.net) where many open source projects flourish. You may even want to get involved with one or two of them.

This chapter gives you an idea of how J2EE provides a great framework for developing applications with XML and databases. In Chapter 8, we took a database-centric approach, building upward from the database and understanding some of the built-in XML functionality that the database can provide. This chapter has been written from the application server perspective—thinking about all the functionality existing in the application server (J2EE or otherwise). Both approaches have relative merits depending on various factors. For instance, if you have a staff of fabulous application programmers, you may want to favor the application-server approach instead of building functionality in the database where your developers' skills aren't as good. On the other hand, if you want your XML database to service many applications written in many different frameworks or platforms, go the database-centric route and hire some ace database programmers.

In Chapter 10, we expand our horizons somewhat and discuss further integration ideas for XML and SQL.

Chapter 10

More Examples: Beyond Silly Web Sites

> In which XML answers the questions: "Where do I live?"
> "What's my phone number?" "How much am I worth?"

For a moment, let's set aside the CyberCinema site examples. (No need to cheer quite so loudly.) XML and relational database systems can be combined for the greater good for other applications besides Web sites, you know. There's a perception out there that XML is "the language of the Internet," and it's true that a lot of XML's application has been related to Internet technologies. But XML is a tool that has other great uses as well.

In this chapter, I present additional, varied examples of how to integrate XML and SQL. I touch on the burgeoning field of Web services, from content management issues to e-commerce.[1] Think of the following as rough design patterns for the applications or modules that you'll be building.

[1.] A Web service doesn't have to exist on the Internet; it can exist on a closed or wide area network. The term *Web service* means the service uses Web technologies (XML and HTTP), not that it actually operates on the Web.

Building a Web Service

If you want to make a data source available to a large number of diverse applications across a network, XML can help you abstract that data source (or process) into a Web service. The idea of a Web service is not new. Although the name *Web service* has come into vogue recently, the idea has been around since the beginning of the Web: Create a program that responds to requests by other programs on a network using HTTP (HyperText Transport Protocol). Web services exclusively use XML to respond to requests, so the client program—the program making the request—just has to be able to decode the XML responses. It doesn't have to know the mechanics behind the service or what the back-end data store is. Hence it can be lighter weight and simpler to write, debug, and deploy. The XML partial decomposition model described primarily in Chapter 6 is great for storing large pieces of unstructured content, but it doesn't lend itself well to applications with more structured, recordlike data.

Corporate Phone Directory

As an example of a Web service, a corporate phone directory is the kind of information that gets updated at a central location and disseminated to other applications that need access to this data. You might keep the information in a SQL database, an LDAP server, or some other data store, but it doesn't really matter as long as you make it available through an XML API to the applications that need it—hence a Web service.

The first step in creating a Web service of this type is to define a simple XML format for your directory information. Let's say we want to expose name and phone number through this interface—an XML instance of a corporate phone directory might look like this:

```
<directory_entry>
    <name>Robert Englund</name>
    <phone>
        <country-code>1</country-code>
        <area-code>212</area-code>
```

```
            <number>555
                <extension>3333</extention>
            </number>
        </phone>
</directory_entry>
```

You can implement a JSP (Java Server Page—see Chapter 9), ASP (Microsoft's Active Server Page), a simple Perl script, or whatever you have that pulls data from your back-end store and responds to HTTP search requests like the following by splitting a piece of XML:

```
http://directoryserver.mycompany.com/getentry?name=Robert
```

With this level of abstraction, you don't really have to worry about which applications access the data. As long as the JSP continues to respond to requests with valid XML, you're all set.

As a bonus, the client applications that access this information don't have to be labored with all the code to access the data store. They therefore can be much lighter weight (for instance, a super lightweight application running on a wireless device). It's also easier and more secure to make this kind of information available through a corporate firewall using an HTTP interface.

Stock Quotes

Let's say you're designing a system that stores an incoming feed of real-time stock pricing information so that other applications can access it. Relational databases aren't really built for this kind of real-time system, so you're going to build something that sits on its own, digesting the feed as it comes in, storing prices internally in memory, and spitting them out to other applications on request. In addition, you want to track historical data. You want to be able to save the high, low, and closing price each day after the closing bell, which sounds like a job for a relational database. The tricky bit is that the real-time feed you're getting sends you only the current price.

First, let's examine the requirements:

- The system must consume a real-time feed of stock prices and store them internally.
- The system must make pricing information (for example, the current price, the 52-week high, the 52-week low, and yesterday's closing price) available to other (external) applications upon request.

Now let's take a quick look at our data model. A stock quote must have the following data fields:

- Stock symbol
- Current price
- 52-week high
- 52-week low
- Yesterday's close
- Date stamp (so we know how fresh the information is)

This isn't a complex data model, but a few interesting technical problems come to mind. First of all, we don't know the nature of these external applications that will be built as consumers of the stock price information. Second, an RDBMS isn't terribly good at being a real-time storage system for information that constantly updates, second-to-second. Finally, the feed itself doesn't contain historical information.

One solution to these problems would be to support interoperability with external applications by implementing a Web service and to store only historical data in the RDBMS. When another application wants a stock quote, it will ask the feed decoder system, which will respond with a stream of XML that might look like this:

```
<STOCK_QUOTE>
<SYMBOL SYMBOL="XYZ"/>
<DATESTAMP DATE="2000-02-18T20:21:07,0"/>
<CURRENT_PRICE PRICE="102.63"/>
<YESTERDAY_CLOSE PRICE="103.72"/>
<FIFTYTWO_HIGH PRICE="117.71"/>
```

```
<FIFTYTWO_LOW PRICE="87.64"/>
</STOCK_QUOTE>
```

However, your relational database schema might look something like this:

```
CREATE TABLE stock_pricing (
    stock       NUMBER(16)   NOT NULL     references some_symbol_table,
    datestamp   TIMEDATE     NOT NULL,
    high        FLOAT(16)    NOT NULL,
    low         FLOAT(16)    NOT NULL,
    close       FLOAT(16)    NOT NULL
);
```

This table gets updated only once per day per stock, after the market closes and final pricing is in. While markets are open and active pricing is coming in over your feed, you're storing the pricing data in a big hash table somewhere in memory. When a request from another program comes in for pricing information, you can grab the current price from memory and get all the historical data from the relational schema.

Again, the power of the relational database is put to use at what it's good at—storing and aggregating large amounts of information. If you want to do historical research about when a particular stock hit its high or use the data to create graphs, the information is all there in the RDBMS.

In this stock quote example, XML is used for one of the things it's good at—transmitting in a standard, generic manner information that can be understood by multiple applications. Your applications on the front end can consume this easy-to-understand XML snippet and display the information in any way they want without having to understand where it came from.

This kind of modular application design also has implications for how the application is developed, enabling geographically separate developers to work together more easily. If you specify what the XML is supposed to look like, you can get one developer working on the feed application and another developer working independently on the system that uses it. One of them can be working in India, the other in Indianapolis.

Using SOAP

SOAP (Simple Object Access Protocol) is a standard for implementing the kind of Web services I've discussed here. It takes the idea of Web services one step further by providing a common XML vocabulary for remote access of information and specifying a few special HTTP headers (metadata that is sent along with an HTTP request or response) that facilitate this kind of interprocess communication. The SOAP standard defines a SOAP envelope (and they accuse *me* of using mixed metaphors), which encapsulates data requests and responses. A SOAP envelope for our stock quote example might look something like this:

```
<?xml version='1.0'?>
<SOAP:Envelope>
 <SOAP:Body>
  <i:getQuote>
   <SYMBOL>CDMS</SYMBOL>
  </i:getQuote>
 </SOAP:Body>
</SOAP:Envelope>
```

The corresponding response might look like this:

```
<?xml version='1.0'?>
<SOAP:Envelope>
 <SOAP:Body>
  <i:QuoteResponse>
   <SYMBOL>CDMS</SYMBOL>
   <DATESTAMP>2000-02-18T20:21:07,0</DATESTAMP>
   <CURRENT_PRICE>10.08</CURRENT_PRICE>
   <YESTERDAY_CLOSE>10.25</YESTERDAY_CLOSE>
   <FIFTYTWO_HIGH PRICE>12.3</FIFTYTWO_HIGH PRICE>
   <FIFTYTWO_LOW>.5</FIFTYTWO_LOW>
  </i:QuoteResponse>
 </SOAP:Body>
</SOAP:Envelope>
```

Of course, you still have to design the XML that goes inside the envelope (the SOAP-specified `<i:…>` tags. The advantage of using SOAP is that—you guessed it—it's another *standard*, and it's quickly being adopted by many of the application server products and data interchange languages. For instance, Java's RMI (Remote Method Invocation) API can be configured to interact with a SOAP data source. So, depending on what external processes must access your data, using SOAP could save you a heck of a lot of time and headache.

SOAP has a big name (Microsoft) behind it as well, so it's not going away any time soon. For a tutorial on SOAP, get *Programming Web Services with SOAP* by James Snell (2001), or take a look at Microsoft's full documentation of the SOAP specification at http://msdn.microsoft.com/library/default.asp?url=/library/en-us/dnsoapsp/html/soapspec.asp.

E-Commerce

In the field of e-commerce where transactions have to occur in real time, it's often advantageous to execute some tasks on the fly and others later in a batch mode. For instance, authorizing a payment on a credit card in real time can be done very quickly, whereas actually fulfilling that payment in real time often takes longer and is more prone to error. If you're running an e-commerce system, you want to be able to process orders as quickly as possible and get the customers out the door or back into your catalog where they can do more purchasing.

Apart from any role XML might play in the transaction between you and your clearing bank, you once again can use XML as the glue between different parts of your application. Your "store" application must be able to keep a record of your order and transmit that information to a payment engine when the customer presses the "Yes, I-Want-It-Now! Now! NOW!" button. (Don't you just love instant gratification?)

Let's consider the data model for such a system, shown in Figure 10-1.

You've got a catalog, that consists of catalog items, and you've got orders that can be comprised of many items and can belong to one customer.

Now, where do you want to use XML here? First of all, because catalog item descriptions are like content, you probably want to use XML to describe your catalog items. These items then can be decomposed into the database in a manner similar to our CyberCinema reviews from the previous chapters. You'll be decomposing item numbers, descriptions, and prices instead of actors and directors. If you want to include graphics (such as a picture of a product in its box) or links in your item descriptions, XML begins to make even more sense.

The interesting new application for XML presented in this example is for the actual order. Say you have two systems: your online catalog and your ordering system. Each has a unique perspective on the world. Your catalog cares about what you sell. Your ordering system cares only about accurately fulfilling orders. XML can bridge these two worlds, providing a common language that both systems can understand and interpret as they want.

An XML instance for an order might look like this:

```
<ORDER ORDER_ID="23402">
<ITEM ITEM_ID="123" PRICE="1.00" CURRENCY_CODE="GBP">
<ITEM_NAME>IRN BRU</ITEM_NAME>
<ITEM_DESCRIPTION>Perplexing Scottish Soft-Drink</ITEM_DESCRIPTION>
</ITEM>
</ORDER>
```

The relational table for the catalog system might look something like this:

```
CREATE TABLE CATALOG_ITEM (
    CATALOG_ITEM_ID NUMERIC NOT NULL,
```

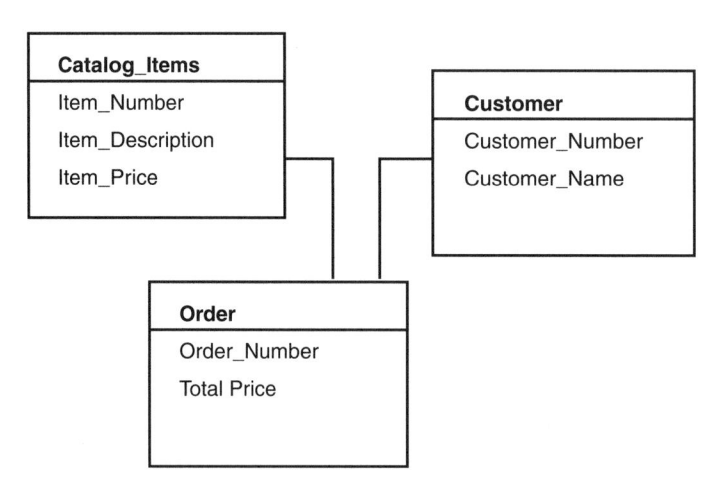

Figure 10-1: Data model diagram for an e-commerce application

```
    CATALOG_ITEM_NAME VARCHAR(128) NOT NULL,
    CATALOG_ITEM_DESCRIPTION VARCHAR(1024)
);
```

And the order fulfillment system might look like this:

```
CREATE TABLE ORDER (
    ORDER_ID NUMERIC NOT NULL,
    ORDER_TOTAL CURRENCY
);
```

By structuring the orders as XML and making XML the transport mechanism between your catalog system and your ordering system, you win in a couple of ways:

- Your display system can show the users their orders without having to grab information from two separate databases and aggregate them.
- The XML orders contain unique IDs from both systems. Given a particular XML order, you can check the order status within the order fulfillment system or cross-reference particular products in the catalog.

If you're designing a generic order fulfillment system that can receive orders and fulfill them from multiple catalogs, this kind of design becomes even more useful (although you'll have to add an additional unique `catalog_id` field into your item element to identify each catalog system uniquely).

Another application of this approach is where you take data from one relational database structure and transfer it to a partner company that then puts the data into its own relational database structure. By using XML as the transport mechanism, you don't have to map data from one database to another or make changes when your partner company changes its data model. You just exchange XML documents so the data models for either company can change as much as they want to, but the XML passed between the companies stays the same. This type of loosely coupled business-to-business (B2B) integration enables businesses to move more quickly because the pace of your own innovation isn't burdened by other businesses' requirements.

Taxonomical Structure

It can be tricky to represent hierarchical information such as taxonomies and their interrelationships to documents using XML. For example, if you have a large corpus of documents, you may want to be able to classify them using hierarchical taxonomies. A *taxonomy* is defined as a division of items (or nodes) into ordered groups or categories. For example, the taxonomy of geographical regions (usually) starts with the Earth and works its way down to things like East Flatbush. A snapshot of your region's taxonomy might look something like the diagram in Figure 10-2.

This kind of structure is what computer scientists call a *graph*. In fact, it's a special kind of graph called a *tree* because each node has one or more child nodes, and every node has only one direct parent node. If we want to capture this taxonomical tree in a relational database each node (in this case, the regions) can be assigned a unique ID number and stored in a schema that might look something like this:

```
CREATE TABLE taxonomy (
    NODE_ID NUMBER NOT NULL,
    PARENT_NODE NUMBER,
```

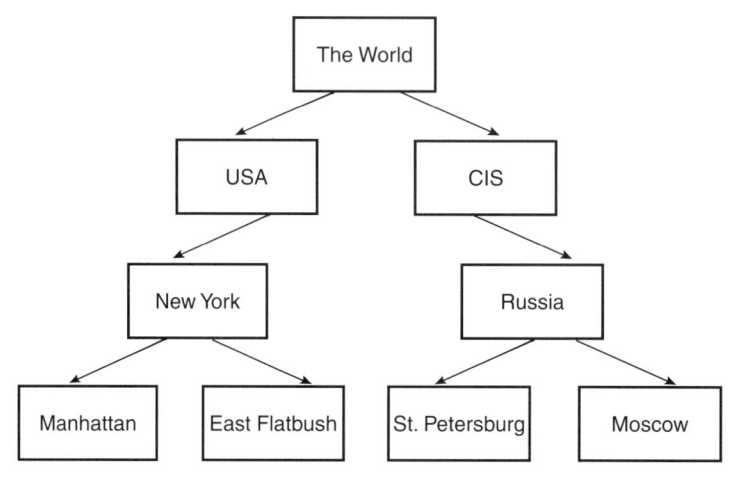

Figure 10-2: Graph of regional taxonomy

```
NODE_NAME VARCHAR(16) NOT NULL
);
```

If you are managing a set of XML documents and you need to keep track of the associations between these documents and the nodes in this taxonomical tree, you quickly run across some complexity because of data consistency issues between your database and your XML documents. You want your XML to be "in the driver's seat," but at the same time, the master record for your taxonomy is in your database.

Depending on the nature of your documents and your desire to label them geographically, you may also want to associate any document with one or more nodes. Your XML document might look something like this:

```
<DOCUMENT>
...
<TAXONOMIES>
<TAXONOMICAL_NODE NODE_ID="123">East Flatbush</TAXONOMICAL_NODE>
<TAXONOMICAL_NODE NODE_ID="273">Moscow</TAXONOMICAL_NODE>
</TAXONOMIES>
...
</DOCUMENT>
```

In this excerpt, the XML instance contains "pointers" into the taxonomical structure. We're not even attempting to mirror the structure of the taxonomy itself, so if Moscow changes from being inside the Soviet Union to being inside the Commonwealth of Independent States, we don't have to change our XML documents—only the database representation of the taxonomy has to change. If you built your XML documents so that they hard-coded the relationship between the taxonomical nodes, you could have a mess on your hands. You would have had to change all those documents when East Germany and West Germany reunited, for instance. If your documents simply contain pointers into the taxonomy (as shown in the preceding example) and the taxonomy itself is stored in the RDBMS, the mess is much smaller.

Another approach to storing taxonomical information in XML instances is to encode the taxonomical structure relevant to the particular nodes you're interested in. This approach is more in line with the Rosetta stone ideas put forth in Chapter 5, but the drawback is that if your taxonomical structure does change, you have to modify all your XML instances to reflect the change. However, if the taxonomies you deal with are fairly static and you're going to be sending your XML to third parties fairly often, you may want to consider this approach.

If you encode the taxonomical structure relevant to the nodes, your SQL schema remains the same. Your XML changes to look something like this:

```
<DOCUMENT>
...
<TAXONOMIES>
  <TAXONOMICAL_NODE NODE_ID="1" NODE_NAME="Earth">
    <TAXONOMICAL_NODE NODE_ID="86" NODE_NAME="USA">
      <TAXONOMICAL_NODE NODE_ID="104" NODE_NAME="New York State">
        <TAXONOMICAL_NODE NODE_ID="123" NODE_NAME="East Flatbush"/>
      </TAXONOMICAL_NODE>
    </TAXONOMICAL_NODE>
    <TAXONOMICAL_NODE NODE_ID="104" NODE_NAME="CIS">
      <TAXONOMICAL_NODE NODE_ID="108" NODE_NAME="Russia">
        <TAXONOMICAL_NODE NODE_ID="273" NODE_NAME="Moscow"/>
      </TAXONOMICAL_NODE>
    </TAXONOMICAL_NODE>
  </TAXONOMICAL_NODE>
</TAXONOMIES>
...
</DOCUMENT>
```

The indentation in the preceding example indicates that this XML fragment represents a hierarchical taxonomy structure. Because both the hierarchy of the nodes and the node ID numbers are preserved in the XML structure, the entire structure can be reconstructed, assuming you have a large enough corpus of documents.

Why is this approach useful or important? Several situations spring to mind. Suppose your database becomes corrupted and is unrecoverable. As long as your XML documents are backed up somewhere, you can recreate the structure of your taxonomy by reimporting the XML documents. Or suppose you're sending your XML as a feed to some third parties (such as portal Web sites) and that third party wants to be able to understand your taxonomical structures so they can build a search or incorporate your keywords into their keywords (portal sites are weird like that). You could create a whole new procedure where you dump your taxonomy structure on a daily basis and send it to them (yet another potential point of failure).

Either way, if the names of the nodes change (for example, the state of North Dakota changes its name to just Dakota), you have to update your XML documents as well as update the information in your RDBMS. When developing systems like this, it's important to build tools that make these kinds of changes easier to implement—in this case, including an administration function to change taxonomical node names and automatically update the corresponding XML files.

LDAP and DSML

An alternative to SQL databases is LDAP (Lighweight Directory Access Protocol). The hierarchical nature of LDAP data stores is particularly well suited to taxonomies and other hierarchical data. If you're dealing with a lot of this kind of data, you might do well to give LDAP a second look. LDAP is not really a competitor to SQL databases. It's a lightweight protocol designed specifically for directory lookups. Because of its light weight, it's particularly well suited for high-volume tasks. The downside, of course, is that even though LDAP is lightweight, if you decide to use it, you're integrating another system into a probably already complex system, and you have to deal with all the issues related to maintaining data integrity between two separate systems. Furthermore, LDAP servers don't do any relational integrity checking or transactions. An open-source LDAP server is available (OpenLDAP, www.openldap.org) as well as several commercial products (most notably Iplanet's Directory Server product, www.iplanet.com/directory).

If you really want to get crazy with the LDAP, you should check out the DSML (Directory Service Markup Language) group at (www.dsml.org). They've built an entire XML framework around LDAP. Their language enables you to specify a directory structure in XML, which maps directly on the capabilities of an LDAP server.

Document Management and Content Locking

Document management systems use the concept of a "workflow state" to track documents as different people work on a document. For instance, a news article might be required to go through several editorial stages before it can be published. The document's life cycle starts with the author creating it and subsequently includes the document being reviewed by an editor and checked by a copy editor. Additional stages are writing a headline and producing graphics for the article. The final stage in a document life cycle is publication. You could write an entire book about designing workflows, but here we're just going to touch on the topic and its relevance to designing a system that uses XML and SQL.

These workflow states can be represented in an RDBMS-based system more effectively than in a purely XML-driven system. A relational schema to represent workflows might look something like this:

```
CREATE TABLE CONTENT (
    CONTENT_ID NUMERIC NOT_NULL,
    CONTENT_XML BLOB NOT_NULL,
    ...whatever else is in your content table...
    CONTENT_WORKFLOW_STATE REFERENCES WORKFLOW_STATE.STATE_ID NOT NULL
    );
CREATE TABLE WORKFLOW (
    STATE_ID NUMERIC NOT NULL,
    STATE_NAME VARCHAR(16) NULT NULL
    );
```

Thus every piece of content gets associated with some workflow state. In a simple content management system where an author writes a document and an editor checks and then publishes it, these states might look like this:

STATE_ID	STATE_NAME
0	AUTHORING
1	EDITING
2	PUBLISHED

Your application is in charge of making sure that no document gets to stage 2 without having first gone through stage 1. You can make the RDBMS help you enforce this requirement: For instance, the RDBMS can start all content with a default workflow state of 0, which means your content changes like this:

```
CREATE TABLE CONTENT (
    CONTENT_ID NUMERIC NOT_NULL,
    CONTENT_XML BLOB NOT_NULL,
    ...whatever else is in your content table...
    CONTENT_WORKFLOW_STATE REFERENCES WORKFLOW_STATE.STATE_ID NOT NULL
        DEFAULT 0
);
```

Now your application doesn't have to worry about setting the workflow state when a new piece of content is created because the new piece of content will be assigned a default state of 0 (with the addition of the DEFAULT 0 clause).

In order to facilitate the editing of content within your workflow, you may want to build in content locking. Content locking becomes especially important when many people (say, more than two) are working together within a workflow system. Again, this type of record-level locking is suited toward a relational database. In this case, a field addition to the content table is all that is needed, relating the content table to a table of system users. The users are the editors of this piece of content; the assumption is that you already have the following user table in your content editing system to facilitate user authentication:

```
CREATE TABLE CONTENT (
    CONTENT_ID NUMERIC NOT_NULL,
    CONTENT_XML BLOB NOT_NULL,
    ...whatever else is in your content table...
    CONTENT_WORKFLOW_STATE REFERENCES WORKFLOW_STATE.STATE_ID NOT NULL
        DEFAULT 0,
    CONTENT_LOCK NUMERIC REFERENCES USER.USER_ID
);
```

Notice that I've left out the "NOT NULL" clause on the definition for CONTENT_LOCK, so null values are allowed here (and the field will default to null when a new piece of content is created). A value of null means that the item isn't locked. Any other value means that the item is locked (and because the value references a row in the user table, that tells you who has the lock).

When a user tries to edit a piece of content, the system must check the condition of the lock for that record. If it isn't locked, the system must lock it (by setting the lock to the user's ID number) and enable the user to edit the XML through whatever means are appropriate. A problem you may run into is where locks conflict. For instance, in a multiuser system, you may have multiple program threads all looking up lock information and trying to lock various items. In the case where one thread checks a lock, find the item to be unlocked. Then, before it can set the lock itself, if the item is locked by another thread, you have a problem. Both threads now think they have a lock on the item, so in the better case, one user's changes are going to override the other's changes. In the worse case, your data may become corrupted or lost. To avoid this situation, you may want to write some embedded SQL (for instance, PL-SQL in Oracle) to check and update the record as part of a single database transaction. In pseudocode, this piece of SQL programming would look something like this:

```
select content_lock from content where content.content_id = whatever_id;
if content_lock is not null
  {
  update content (content_lock) values (your_user_id)
      where content.content_id = whatever_id;
  select content_xml from content where content.content_id = whatever_id;
  }
else
  {
  return to the application some indication that the record is locked
  }
```

The idea is to push as much functionality back into the database as you can. This increases the efficiency of your application because it doesn't have to do multiple selects (first to determine the state of the lock and then actually to get the content). It also ensures that no one can go in and change the state of the lock between the time you check it and the time you update it.

WebDav: Web-based Distributed Authoring and Versioning

Those of you really excited about document management might want to check out the WebDav project at www.webdav.org. WebDav, in its creator's own words, "is a set of extensions to the HTTP protocol which allows users to collaboratively edit and manage files on remote Web servers." That essentially means that the folks at WebDav have built some extensions to the HTTP protocol to facilitate document management. Microsoft, in an article written in March 2000 (http://msdn.microsoft.com/xml/articles/xmlandwebdav.asp), calls WebDav "an important communication protocol for the Web." They go on to describe a very compelling integration between XML and WebDav.

WebDav uses XML for storage of metadata, but you can imagine a SQL-back-ended, WebDav-based authoring system that uses partial decomposition to store and keep track of this metadata, which is especially useful for reporting purposes when you need to look up the history of a particular piece of content.

WebDav is starting to make inroads in some mainstream technologies as well. WebDav is enabled in both the latest version of the Microsoft Windows operating system and Apple's new OS X.

Versioning and Change Management

The concept of versioning is closely linked to workflow. Document versioning, when properly implemented, can enable a user to step back in time to previous versions of a document, tracking not only how, but by whom, a document was modified. Understandably, this kind of obsessive document management is popular with lawyers and is in use by many publishers as well. If you're dealing with legal contracts, you might be interested in when particular paragraphs or clauses were amended and by whom. Likewise, if your content management system tracks these changes for you, it makes it difficult to make changes to documents without the proper authorization. Hook up this document management system to a workflow system, like the one we described earlier, and you're really cooking with gas.

LegalXML

The LegalXML working group (www.legalxml.org) has set about to define an open, nonproprietary standard for representation of legal documents in XML format. It's not rocket science; basically we're talking about stuff like this:

```
<Legal>
  <Contract>
    <Title>Employment Contract</Title>
    <Clause>Employee will do work for Employer</Clause>
    <Clause>Employer will pay Employee</Clause>
  </Contract>
<Legal>
```

You can see where this effort will end up. Automated judge machines will someday replace the entire civil court system by parsing and evaluating contracts against claims. All claims not submitted in valid LegalXML will be summarily thrown out. Malformed tags will be grounds for dismissal. Remember: You heard it here first.

Versioning usually works like this: Whenever you edit a document from the document management system and then save your changes, the old document is not overwritten. If you're storing your XML documents in the RDBMS, a new row is inserted into the table, and the newly changed document is inserted there, along with some information about the person modifying it and when the change took place.

Building from our previous example, a content table with versioning looks like this:

```
CREATE TABLE CONTENT (
    CONTENT_ID NUMERIC NOT_NULL,
    CONTENT_VERSION NUMERIC NOT_NULL DEFAULT 0,
    CONTENT_TIMESTAMP DATETIME NOT_NULL,
    CONTENT_WHOLAST NUMERIC REFERENCES USER.USER_ID,
```

```
CONTENT_XML BLOB NOT_NULL,
...whatever else is in your content table...
CONTENT_WORKFLOW_STATE REFERENCES WORKFLOW_STATE.STATE_ID NOT NULL
    DEFAULT 0,
CONTENT_LOCK NUMERIC REFERENCES USER.USER_ID
);
```

We've added a VERSION column to the content table as a simple numeric that can be incremented whenever a new version is created (with a default of 0). The TIMESTAMP field holds the date and the time this version was saved, and the WHOLAST field stores the identity of the editor (again, referencing the user table). You may also want to add a version element to your XML so that you can tell what version you're looking at within the XML file itself. You can do so by simply adding a VERSION attribute to your root document element:

```
<DOCUMENT VERSION="23">
...content of document...
</DOCUMENT>
```

Now whenever the system needs the latest version, it can provide it by selecting the one with the greatest version number (which again is a function the database can perform quite easily). Likewise, it can enable a user to step through all the previous versions but allow edits only to the latest version.

Summary

In this chapter, I've introduced some examples of further applications for XML and SQL. The concept of a Web service, in particular, is one you can apply to any of the subjects covered in this book and is a key enabling technology for the kind of business transformation that I talked about in the Introduction. The ability for businesses to interact with each other, through global networks, using "loosely coupled" technology such as Web services will also be an accelerator for those businesses. It will make the technology they rely on simpler and more modular and thereby make it easier for business to evolve and innovate, that is, to move faster. The techniques discussed in this book for integrating XML and SQL can help to make these types of services more robust and allow them to plug more easily into existing systems.

Many of the concepts discussed in this book and, in particular, the concepts of workflow, content locking, and change management discussed in this chapter, are useful in the field of content management. *Content management* is an industry buzzword, and as with any industry buzzword, the definition varies depending on what whoever uses it is trying to sell you. I've been a director of content management, and I've done content management consulting, but I was doing content management before there was a content management.

Now you can buy pieces of software that claim to be "content management systems." Many of these systems are quite good at what they do—provide a development environment for building content management applications. Most of the content management systems involve some kind of integration between XML and SQL, and many of them claim to be able to do all sorts of things (like make toast) "out of the box." But because a packaged application has to take a one-size-fits-all approach, it necessarily is more than you need.

As I indicated in Chapter 3, I highly recommend developing a set of business requirements, building a data model, and even a DTD before selecting tools. This goes *double* for so-called content management systems. Figure out *what you need*; then take a look at the tools that are available, and figure out how far those tools go toward satisfying your requirements and what the trade-offs of using them are. For instance, I selected a toolkit for TheStreet.com that I knew would help us develop quickly to reach a hard deadline, but the trade-off was that the development language wasn't my language of choice. Don't let vendors drive your requirements with their marketing messages. Examine these tools for what they are and what functionality they provide before you select one.

I hope reading this book has been as much fun for you as writing it has been for me. Writing this book has been therapeutic in more ways than one. The impetus for starting it was that I thought many people misunderstood the power that XML could bring to their applications and the ways in which XML could be integrated with SQL-based systems to build powerful applications. In this book, I've provided my viewpoint, based on personal experience, of an approach to XML and the integration of XML and SQL that works and that can help you build applications that meet and exceed business needs. I've also outlined an approach to building applications that I think works, especially for the scale of applications that we've covered in this book. Larger, more complex applications may need a more rigorous, more structured approach, but before you go down that road, ask yourself if the system you are building can be "componentized" into smaller, more easily developed and maintained "chunks" that integrate using the Web services ideas presented in this chapter. Above all, keep it simple, and keep it documented. And if I leave you with nothing else, think of quality assurance and testing at every step of your development process.

Appendix

This appendix contains the fully formed DTD for our CyberCinema example, annotated with comments. As discussed in Chapter 5, this DTD splits our movie review documents up into a HEAD section and a BODY section. The HEAD section contains all the record-like data (such as the title, the date of publication, and the author information), and the BODY contains the actual text of the review. The text stylings (such as `<I>` for italics) have been borrowed from XHTML for simplicity. Such stylings are also convenient if you happen to be transforming to a delivery format of XHTML, or an XHTML variant, because you don't have to transform those tags that are already XTML tags.

Also note at the front of this DTD the use of XML entities to define content models (particularly `%flow;`) that are then used throughout the rest of the DTD—where other elements are defined. The `%flow;` entity definition itself is comprised of other entity definitions and `%PCDATA` (parseable character data).

```
<!DOCTYPE moviereview.1 SYSTEM "moviereview.dtd" [
<!—

This is the full DTD for movie reviews for the fictitious CyberCinema
movie review site.

Version 1.0

*** 22 August 2001
If all your changes are commented here, it will make the DTD
```

easier to understand when reading it for the first time.

*** 21 August 2001

A good idea is to have a version log at the top of your DTD in a comment block like this one.

*** 20 August 2001

Tomorrow I will write another comment above.

—>

<!—

Pull in the regular entity definition for HTML, which includes things like the British pound sign

—>

<!ENTITY % HTMLlat1 PUBLIC
   "-//W3C//ENTITIES Latin 1 for XHTML//EN"
   "xhtml-lat1.ent">
%HTMLlat1;

<!ENTITY % HTMLsymbol PUBLIC
   "-//W3C//ENTITIES Symbols for XHTML//EN"
   "xhtml-symbol.ent">
%HTMLsymbol;

<!ENTITY % HTMLspecial PUBLIC
   "-//W3C//ENTITIES Special for XHTML//EN"
   "xhtml-special.ent">
%HTMLspecial;

<!—

Define entities for some of the content models we will be using in the rest of the DTD. That way, we can change these one place (up here) and change the content models for many of the elements below

—>

```
<!ENTITY % fontstyle "I | B | U | SUB | SUP | BR">

<!ENTITY % special "MOVIE | REVIEW | PERSON">

<!ENTITY % list "UL | OL">

<!ENTITY % flow "(#PCDATA | %fontstyle; | %phrase; | %special;)*">

<!- The main root element for our reviews ->

<!ELEMENT CYBERCINEMA_REVIEW (HEAD, BODY)>

<!- Definition of the HEAD element and the contents thereof ->

<!ELEMENT HEAD (REVIEWED, HEADLINE, ABSTRACT, CREATE_DATE, LASTMOD_DATE, PUBLISH_DATE)>

<!- REVIWED TAG contains ID number of the movie being reviewed in this review ->

<!ELEMENT REVIEWED EMPTY>

<!ATTLIST REVIEWED
          ID                        NMTOKEN           #REQUIRED
>


<!- Author block where list of authors is found ->

<!ELEMENT AUTHOR_BLOCK (AUTHOR*)>

<!- Each individual author ->

<!ELEMENT AUTHOR (#CDATA)>

<!ATTLIST AUTHOR
```

```
                ID              NMTOKEN         #REQUIRED
>

<!-- The headline and abstract -->

<!ELEMENT HEADLINE (%flow;)*>

<!ELEMENT ABSTRACT (%flow;)*>


<!-- The create date, last modified date and publish date of this
     review -->

<!ELEMENT CREATE_DATE #CDATA>

<!ATTLIST CREATE_DATE
            DATE            CDATA           #REQUIRED
>

<!ELEMENT LASTMOD_DATE #CDATA>

<!ATTLIST LASTMOD_DATE
            DATE            CDATA           #REQUIRED
>

<!ELEMENT PUBLISH_DATE #CDATA>

<!ATTLIST PUBLISH_DATE
            DATE            CDATA           #REQUIRED
>

<!-- Definition of the BODY element and the contents thereof -->

<!ELEMENT BODY (%flow;)*>

<!-- For centering text -->
```

```
<!ELEMENT CENTER (%flow;)*>

<!— Paragraph tag, for enclosing paragraphs —>

<!ELEMENT P (%flow;)*>

<!— Supersubscript and Subscript —>

<!ELEMENT (SUB|SUP) (%flow;)*>

<!— Empty tag to insert line breaks in text —>

<!ELEMENT BR EMPTY>

<!—
Lists we'll allow in this DTD.  Ordered lists and unordered
lists.  Again, this is pulled from HTML definition
—>

<!— Ordered lists (OL) Numbering style —>
<!ENTITY % OLStyle "CDATA"       — constrained to: "(1|a|A|i|I)" —>

<!ELEMENT OL - - (LI)+              — ordered list —>
<!ATTLIST OL
   type         %OLStyle;      #IMPLIED  — numbering style —
   compact      (compact)      #IMPLIED  — reduced interitem spacing —
   start        NUMBER         #IMPLIED  — starting sequence number —
   >

<!— Unordered Lists (UL) bullet styles —>
<!ENTITY % ULStyle "(disc|square|circle)">

<!ELEMENT UL - - (LI)+              — unordered list —>
<!ATTLIST UL
   type         %ULStyle;      #IMPLIED  — bullet style —
   compact      (compact)      #IMPLIED  — reduced interitem spacing —
   >
```

```
<!ELEMENT LI - O (%flow;)**           -- list item -->
<!ATTLIST LI
    type        %LIStyle;   #IMPLIED  -- list item style --
    value       NUMBER      #IMPLIED  -- reset sequence number --
    >


<!-- Our links for movies, people and other reviews -->

<!ELEMENT MOVIE (%flow;)*>

<!ATTLIST MOVIE
        xlink:type      (simple|extended|locator|arc)   #FIXED "locator"

        <!-- This is a locator link because it points to an external resource -->

                xlink:href          NMTOKEN             #REQUIRED
                xlink:show                              (new | embed | replace)    "replace"

        <!-- When link is actuated (such as with a click) should the linked-to
             data come up in a new window, be embedded in the current window or
             replace the current content? -->

             xlink:actuate      (onRequest |onLoad)     "onRequest"
             <!-- How should the link be activated? Default is on user request -->
>

<!ELEMENT REVIEW (%flow;)*>

<!ATTLIST REVIEW
        xlink:type      (simple|extended|locator|arc)   #FIXED "locator"

        <!-- This is a locator link because it points to an external resource -->

            xlink:href          NMTOKEN                 #REQUIRED
            xlink:show                      (new | embed | replace)    "replace"
```

        <!— When link is actuated (such as with a click) should the linked-to
            data come up in a new window, be embedded in the current window or
            replace the current content? —>

        xlink:actuate   (onRequest |onLoad)   "onRequest"
        <!— How should the link be activated? Default is on user request —>
>

<!ELEMENT PERSON (%flow;)*>

<!ATTLIST PERSON
        xlink:type   (simple|extended|locator|arc)   #FIXED "locator"

        <!— This is a locator link because it points to an external resource —>

        xlink:href   NMTOKEN   #REQUIRED
        xlink:show   (new | embed | replace)   "replace"

        <!— When link is actuated (such as with a click) should the linked-to
            data come up in a new window, be embedded in the current window or
            replace the current content? —>

        xlink:actuate   (onRequest |onLoad)   "onRequest"
        <!— How should the link be activated? Default is on user request —>
>

]>

Bibliography

Books

XML: A Manager's Guide by Kevin Dick (Reading, Mass.: Addison-Wesley; 1999)

SQL Queries for Mere Mortals: A Hands-On Guide to Data Manipulation in SQL by Michael J. Hernandez (Boston, Mass.: Addison-Wesley, 2000)

That's Not What I Meant: How Conversational Style Makes or Breaks Relationships by Deborah Tannen (New York: Ballantine Books, 1991)

Use Case Driven Object Modeling With UML: A Practical Approach by Doug Rosenberg and Kendall Scott (Reading, Mass.: Addison-Wesley, 1999)

Extreme Programming Explained by Kent Beck (Boston, Mass.: Addison-Wesley, 2000)

Just XML by John E. Simpson (Upper Saddle River, New Jersey: Prentice Hall, 2000)

XML and Java: Developing Web Applications by Hiroshi Maruyama, Kent Tamura, and Naohiko Uramoto (Reading, Mass.: Addison-Wesley, 1999)

Programming Web Services with SOAP by James Snell (O'Reilly & Associates: Sebastopal, Cal., 2001)

XML in a Nutshell by Elliotte Rusty Harold & W. Scott Means (O'Reilly & Associates: Sebastopal, Cal., 2000)

Web Sites

www.iso.ch: The International Standards Organization

www.w3.org: The World Wide Web Consortium

www.xml.com: O'Reilly's XML Portal

www.xml.org: XML Portal maintained by the Oasis group

www.softwareqatest.com: The Software QA/Test Resource Center

www.dsdm.org: Dynamic Systems Development Method Consortium

www.extremeprogramming.org: Extreme Programming HQ

www.ganthead.com: IT Project Management Portal and Resource Center

java.sun.com/xml/: Sun's pages for information on use of XML with Java

www.sourceforge.net: Open-Source project repository and community portal

Index

& (ampersand), 69-70, 138
/ (forward slash), 76
< (less-than symbol), 69
@ (percent sign), 137
+ (plus sign), 137
; (semicolon), 69

A

ABSTRACT element, 118
Abstraction layer, 175
Active user involvement, 42
ADO (Microsoft Active Data Objects), 134
Algorithms, data encoding, 84
Allaire JRun, 176
Amaya browser, 24. *See also* Browsers
American Express, xvii-xviii
ANSI (American National Standards Institute), 22
AOL (America Online), 23
Apache, 106, 176
Application(s). *See also* Application program interfaces (APIs)
 building, essential steps to, 9-10
 -centric thinking, 57
 data-oriented design of, 50-51
 development cycle for, 28
 "killer," 18
 supporting a wide variety of, as a design goal, 15
Application program interfaces (APIs), 180, 184
 JAXP (Java API for XML Processing), 158, 159-160, 162, 165-166, 171-172
 JDBC (Java DataBase Connection API), 134, 158-159, 162-163, 165, 172-175
 SAX (Simple API for XML), 158-160, 163-165
Archeologists, 64, 66-68
Arrays
 basic description of, 21
 multidimensional, 21
 SQL data maps and, 22-23
Art Technology Group, 176
ASCII (American Standard Code for Information Interchange), 137
ASP (Microsoft Active Server Pages), 158

211

Astra, 42
ATG Dynamo, 176
ATTLIST keyword, 71
Attribute(s)
  basic description of, 19, 64
  IDs, 67–68
  list declarations, 71
  semantically encoded links and, 111–112
  XLink and, 80
Audio CDs (compact discs), 4–5
AUTO mode, 132–133, 146, 147

B
<b> tag, 70
B2B (business-to-business) communications, xviii–xix
B2E (business-to-employee) communications, xix
Bandwidth, 17–18
base64 encoding, 84
BEA WebLogic, 176
Beck, Kent, 45
Berners-Lee, Tim, 12
Binary data. *See also* BLOBs (Binary Large Objects)
  arbitrary, dealing with, 83–85
  encoding, 84
  formats, 16
  pointing to, externally, 83
BLOBs (Binary Large Objects), 174–175
Body. *See also* BODY element
  XLink and, 79–82
  XML instance, 78–85
BODY element, 69, 70, 125. *See also* Body

Boldface font, 3, 13, 94
Bray, Tim, 80, 111
Bridging tables, 21, 103–104
Browsers. *See also* Internet Explorer browser (Microsoft)
  HTTP and, 134
  links and, 79, 105–107
  URLs and, 137
  XHTML and, 85

 tag, 85
Bugs. *See also* Errors
  schema and, 102
  tracking, 41
Bugzilla, 41

C
C++ (high-level language), 158
Caching, 98–100, 171–172
Carlson, David, 38
Carriage returns, 74
CDATA (character data), 53, 69, 78
CDs (compact discs), 4–5
Census Bureau (United States), 50
CERN (European Center for Particle Physics), 12
Change management, 195–197
Character. *See also* CLOB (Character Large Object)
  data (CDATA), 53, 69, 78
  entities, 69–70
  sets, 70
CHAR data type, 93
Class(es)
  data modeling and, 57
  DTDs as, 66
CLOB (Character Large Object), 93, 97, 174–175

Index

Code
  commenting, 71
  hard-coding, 6
Collaborative filtering, 110
Comments, 71
Communication styles, 34–35
Complexity, 58–60
Concise, use of the term, 17
Constitutional law, 11
Constraint(s)
  integrity, 98
  management, 95, 96, 98
Content authors, 112–113
Content model, 69, 74, 79, 201
Conversational style, 34–35
Corporate phone directory, 180–181
CREATE TABLE statement, 93, 96–98, 103
Customer(s)
  developers and, disconnect between, 42
  requirements gathering and, 27–29
CyberCinema Web site
  adding media to, 59–60
  basic description of, 29–30
  data modeling and, 49–61
  decomposing, 100–113
  DTD design and, 72–87, 201–207
  functional requirements document for, 35–38
  requirements gathering techniques and, 30–35
  schema and, 91–114
  user scenarios and, 30–33

D
Data
  binding, basic description of, 175
  -centric approaches, 50–54
  future-proofing, notion of, 2–3, 68
  integrity, 90
  management utilities, 99
Data types. *See also* Data types (listed by name)
  attributes and, 19
  data modeling and, 53
  JDBC, 174–175
  SQL, 93
Data types (listed by name). *See also* Data types
  CHAR data type, 93
  DATE data type, 103
  TEXT data type, 93
  varchar data type, 53, 93
Date(s)
  create dates, 75
  data type for, 103
  DTDs and, 75, 77–78
  last modified dates, 75
  schema design and, 103
  standards for, 77
  two-digit, 17
  use of the term, 75
  Y2K issues and, 17
DBAs (database administrators), 68, 97
Decomposition
  basic description of, 7, 95
  caching and, 171
  cautions for using, 83
  of the CyberCinema Web site, 100–113
  data synchronization and, 99
  link management and, 107–108

partial, 94–100
problems with, 100
semantically encoded links and, 111–112
using SAX events to drive, 163–165
De facto standards, 24
DefaultHandler class, 163
De jure standards, 24
DELETE statement, 154
Dick, Kevin, xiv
Disaster
 -proofing, 68
 recovery, 92
Document(s). *See also* DOM (Document Object Model); DTDs (document type definitions)
 future-proofing, 2–3, 68
 requirements, 35–42, 58, 59
 working with, 152–154
DocumentBuilder object, 162
<document> tag, 8
DOM (Document Object Model)
 basic description of, 159–160
 building Java objects for XML instances with, 161–162
 parser, 154, 158–160, 167
Domain-specific languages, 116
DSDM (Dynamic Systems Development Method), 42–43, 45
DSML (Directory Service Markup Language), 191
DTDs (document type definitions)
 archives for, 86
 basic description of, 63–66
 building, 66–72, 85–86
 comments and, 71
 CyberCinema Web site and, 72–87, 201–207
 data-oriented design and, 52
 link management and, 107
 processing without, 14–15
 schema and, 91, 100, 101, 121–126
 SQL Server and, 142
 XML Views and, 142
Dummy files, creating, 67

E
Ease-of-use, importance if, 34
Easy recall, organizing data for, 96–98
E-business, 26–27, 185–188
EDI (Electronic Data Interchange), 117
Editors, 65
E-Doc, 1–2
EJBs (Enterprise Java Beans)
 basic description of, 158, 166–170
 JDBC and, 172–175
 persistence of, 174
ELEMENT keyword, 69
Elements. *See also* Elements (listed by name); Tags
 basic description of, 64
 empty, 76
 organizing, within blocks, 75–78
Elements (listed by name). *See also* Elements
 ABSTRACT element, 118
 BODY element, 69, 70, 125
 FROM element, 69
 HEAD element, 74–78, 125
 MOVIE element, 81, 107, 125
 PERSON element, 81, 107, 125
 REVIEW element, 81, 125

SUBJECT element, 69, 70
TO element, 69
ElementType definition, 151
E-mail systems, 40, 96–99
   building DTDs for, 68–72
   data modeling and, 52–54
   fields for, 52–53, 60, 67, 68, 71
   numerical ID numbers and, 67–68
   requirements and, 27–29
   schema and, 91–114
Emergent property, use of the term, xviii–xix
<em> tag, 13, 14, 118–119
ENC (Environment Naming Context), 173
endDocument method, 163
endElement method, 163
Entity
   references, 69–70
   relationship diagrams, 54
   sets, 69–70
Errors. *See also* Bugs
   dead link, 105
   decomposition and, 98
   URLs and, 105, 137
Essential use cases, 37. *See also* Use cases
Expectations, managing, 27
EXPLICIT mode, 132–134, 146
Extreme programming (XP), 43–45
Extreme Programming Explained (Beck), 45

F

Fields, for e-mail messages, 52–53, 60, 67, 68, 71
Filtering, collaborative, 110

Flags, 83
Flash (Macromedia), 24
Fonts, 3, 70, 94, 201
FOR XML AUTO clause, 132–133
FOR XML clause, 131–132, 136, 146, 147
FOR XML EXPLICIT clause, 133–134, 143
Founding Fathers, 11
FROM element, 69
Functionality, 90
Future-proofing, notion of, 2–3, 68

G

GIF (Graphics Interchange Format), 16, 24, 84–85
GML (Generalized Markup Language), 12, 22
GMT (Greenwich Mean Time), 77–78
Granularity, 40
Graph, use of the term, 188
Groupthink, avoiding, 34
GSM (Global System for Mobile Communications), 18

H

Hard-coding, 6
HEAD element, 74–78, 125
Hernandez, Michael J., x
Hexadecimal notation, 137
Hollerith, Herman, 50
Homer, 5–6, 9, 13, 23
Horizontal rules, 13
HTML (HyperText Markup Language), 9, 12–14
   binary data and, 83–84
   BODY element and, 79

compatibility of XML with, 14
data modeling and, 59
eXtensible (XHTML), 84–85, 118, 119, 201
links and, 79
page generation and, 171
SGML as the foundation of, 2, 12
shortcomings of, 3–5
HTTP (HyperText Transfer Protocol)
  headers, 184
  POST method, 141, 143
  requests, 158, 165, 181
  retrieving data in XML format and, 130–131
  SOAP envelopes and, 184
  SQL Server and, 134–136
  WebDav and, 195
  Web services and, 180, 181
  XSLT and, 165

I

IBM (International Business Machines), 22, 125, 127, 176
ICE (Information Content Exchange), 116
IIS (Microsoft Internet Information Server), 134, 135–136
Immigrant-tracking systems, 50, 51
Inactive flags, 83
Informix, 93
INNER JOIN keyword, 20
INSERT statement, 154
Instances
  basic description of, 19, 65–66
  building DTDs and, 68–72
  building Java objects for, 161–162
  deleting, 83

dummy XML, 63–64
partial decomposition and, 95–99
thinking like an archeologist and, 66–67, 68
validation of, 65–66
Integration testing, 39–42
Integrity, data, 90, 95, 98, 104–105, 109
Internet Explorer browser (Microsoft), 137, 138, 140. *See also* Browsers
Interoperability, 182
Intranets, 130–131
ISAPI (Internet Server API), 136
ISBN (International Standard Book Number), 6–9, 23–24
ISO (International Standards Organization), 12, 16, 22
  basic description of, 23–24
  date formats and, 77
  ratification of standards by, 24
<i> tag, 70
Italic font, 3, 70, 79, 201

J

J2EE (Java 2 Enterprise Edition), 158, 166
  application servers, 175–176
  basic description of, 157
  JAXP and, 159
  unit testing and, 39
Jacquard, Joseph Marie, 50, 51
Jakarta Project, 176
Java. *See also* J2EE (Java 2 Enterprise Edition)
  API for XML Processing (JAXP), 158, 159–160, 162, 165–166, 171–172

DataBase Connection API (JDBC), 134, 158–159, 162–163, 165, 172–175
  data binding and, 175
  data modeling and, 53
  dealing with XML in, 159–172
  Naming and Directory Interface (JNDI), 172–175
  objects, building, 161–162
  OPENXML and, 153
  platform-dependence and, 10
  programming, overview of, 157–177
  transformation mechanisms and, 165–166, 171–172
  unit testing and, 39
JavaScript, 148
JavaSoft, 175
JavaWorld, 176
JAXP (Java API for XML Processing), 158, 159–160, 162, 165–166, 171–172
JDBC (Java DataBase Connection API), 134, 158–159, 162–163, 165, 172–175
JNDI (Java Naming and Directory Interface), 172–175
Joins, 20
Just XML (Simpson), 87

K
"Killer applications," 18
King Gustav Adolphus II (King of Sweden), 25–27, 45

L
Latin 1 character set, 70

LDAP (Lightweight Directory Access Protocol), 180, 191
LegalXML, 196
Lexical analysis, 109–110
Link(s). *See also* URLs (Uniform Resource Locators)
  dead, 105
  maintaining the integrity of, 171
  management, 105–113
  "rot," problem of, 105, 106
  schema design and, 105–113
  semantically-encoded, 112–113
  XLink and, 79–82
localName parameter, 164
Logic, 51, 92, 97

M
Macromedia Flash, 24
Management, of projects
  basic description of, 25–45
  DSDM (Dynamic Systems Development Method) and, 42–43
  technical specification documents and, 45–46
  XP (extreme programming) and, 43–45
Mars Climate Orbiter, 39
Maruyama, Hiroshi, 158
Memory. *See also* Caching
  CLOBs and, 97
  OPENXML and, 154
  storing stock quotes in, 181
Mercury Interactive, 42
Meta data, basic description of, 5
Microsoft ADO (Active Data Objects), 134

Microsoft ASP (Active Server Pages), 158
Microsoft IIS (Internet Information Server), 134, 135–136
Microsoft Internet Explorer browser, 137, 138, 140. *See also* Browsers
Microsoft SQL Server
  basic description of, 129–158
  Books Online, 136, 139
  communicating with, over the Web, 134–136
  DTDs and, 142
  extensions, architecture of, 135–136
  FOR XML AUTO clause, 132–133
  FOR XML clause, 131–132, 136, 146, 147
  FOR XML EXPLICIT clause, 133–134, 143
  Query Analyzer, 134, 148
  retrieving data in XML format and, 130–134, 136–144
  schema and, 93
  template files and, 138–141
  working with XML documents and, 152–154
  XML Views and, 141–146
Microsoft Visual Basic, 148, 153
Microsoft Web sites, 23, 149
Microsoft Windows NT, 10
Model(s). *See also* Modeling
  adding media and, 59–60
  complexity and, 58–60
  defining relationships for, 56
  entity relationship diagrams and, 54
  many-to-many relationships and, 58–59, 60
  many-to-one relationships and, 58–59, 60
  schema and, 90–92
Modeling. *See also* Models
  basic description of, 49–62
  CyberCinema Web site and, 54–60
  data-centric approaches and, 50–54
  examining requirements for, 53
  simplicity and, 56–58
  visualization techniques and, 54
Modeling XML Applications with UML: Practical e-Business Applications (Carlson), 38
MOVIE element, 81, 107, 125
Mozilla, 41
MQ Series, 117
Multichannel publishing models, x
Multidimensional arrays, 21
Multimodal world, xii–xiii
Music, publishing, 4–5
MXSML parser, 154
MySQL, 10, 93

N
Namespaces, 164
namespaceURI parameter, 164
Naming conventions, 40
NASA Mars Climate Orbiter, 39
Netherlands, 23
Nodes, addressing, 120
Normalization, 56
Notation, 137
Numerical IDs, 67, 93–94, 106

O

Object(s)
building, 161–162
ID numbers, 106
large, 92, 174–175
-oriented programming (OOP), 57, 66
schema as a collection of, 89
storage of, 92
Odyssey (Homer), 5–6, 9, 13, 23
OpenXML, 136, 152–154
OPENXML clause, 136
OPENXML keyword, 152–154
Oracle, 89, 93
XML Schema and, 125
XQuery and, 127

P

Pagers, 4, 18
Pair programming, 44
Parameters, 139–140, 164
Parsers
DOM, 154, 158–160, 167
MXSML, 154
OPENXML and, 154
optional features and, 16
regular expressions and, 117
white space and, 74
PCDATA (parseable character data), 69, 78, 201
PDF (Portable Document Format), 16
Performance analysis, 100
Persistent parse tree schema, 94
Perl, 4, 6
Java as an alternative to, 157
platform-dependence and, 10
regular expressions and, 117
PERSON element, 81, 107, 125
Phone directory, corporate, 180–181
Photons, 22
Platform-dependence, 10
Plural, use of, 75–78
Practical Information Architecture: A Hands-On Approach to Structuring Successful Websites (Reiss), 35
Problem tracking, 41
Processing layer, 92
Programming Web Services with SOAP (Snell), 185
Projects
definition of, 25–42
management of, 25–45
Prototypes, 43, 44
Pseudo-SQL, 93
<p> tag, 13, 85, 118–119
Punch-card systems, 50, 51

Q

Quality assurance (QA), 38–42
Queries
basic description of, 126–128
FOR XML clause and, 131–132
FOR XML EXPLICIT clause and, 132–134
HTTP POST method and, 141
with parameters, 139–140
semantically-encoded links and, 112
simple, 9
tracking books by ISBN and, 9
in URLs, 137–138
XPath and, 141
Query Analyzer, 134, 148

R

RAD (Rapid Application Development), 42
Rational Rose, 38
RAW mode, 132, 133, 146
RDBMS (relational database management system). *See also* Relational databases
   advantages of, 7–8
   content locking and, 192–195
   document management and, 192–195
   schema and, 94
   storing only historical data in, 182, 183
   taxonomical systems and, 189, 191
   workflow states and, 192–193
RDF (Resource Description Framework), 111
Readability, 16
References
   basic description of, 19, 21
   current, maintaining, 82–83
   differentiating, 107–108
Referential integrity, 8, 21–22
Regular expressions, 117
Reiss, Erich L., 35
Relational databases. *See also* RDBMS (relational database management system)
   basic description of, 19–20
   referential integrity and, 21–22
   schema design and, 89–114
Relationships
   defining, 56
   many-to-many, 58–59, 60
   many-to-one, 58–59, 60

Replication, 92
REQUIRED keyword, 71
Requirements
   communication styles and, 34–35
   data modeling and, 52–53, 58, 59
   documents, 35–42, 58, 59
   DTDs and, 72
   examining, 53
   extreme programming and, 43–44
   how to capture, 27–29, 30–35
   quality assurance and, 38–42
   scope creep and, 26
   use of the term, 27
   user scenarios and, 30–33
Research in Motion, 4
Reserved symbols, 70
Reverse-proxy caches, 172. *See also* Caching
REVIEW element, 81, 125
Rosenberg, Doug, 38
Rosetta stone, 64, 66, 72

S

SAP, 125
SAX (Simple API for XML)
   basic description of, 159–160
   events, using, to drive XML partial decomposition, 163–165
   parser, 158–160
Schema
   as alternatives to DTDs, 121–126
   annotated, 142–143
   basic description of, 89–115, 121–126
   bridging tables and, 102–105
   caching strategies and, 98–99
   dates and, 103

DTDs and, 73
link management and, 105–113
numerical ID numbers and, 67
partial decomposition and, 94–100
for templates, 139–140
XDR and, 142–143
XML storage and, 93
Scope creep, 26, 42, 43
Scott, Kendall, 38
SDS (Special Delivery Services), xvii
Security, 134–135
SELECT statement, 131
Semantic Web, notion of, 111
Server(s)
CLOBs and, 97
HTTP POST queries and, 141
IIS (Microsoft Internet Information Server), 134, 135–136
J2EE-compliant, 157
LDAP, 180, 191
page-caching, 172
rewriting URLs on, 106
security, 134–135
-side Java, 157–158
virtual directories and, 136
Servlets, 165
SGML (Standard Generalized Markup Language)
compatibility of XML with, 15, 16
DTDs and, 15, 63
lessons of, 1–3
optional features and, 16
XML as a form of, 3, 12–13
Simplicity, importance of, 56–58
Simpson, John, 87
Singular, use of, 75–78
Snell, James, 195

SOAP (Simple Object Access Protocol), 184–185
Software QA/Test Resource Center, 41
Sony, 23
Spaces, 74
SQL (Structured Query Language), 7, 157–177. *See also* Queries; SQL Server (Microsoft)
data types, 93
history of, 11–24
partial decomposition and, 95–96
pseudo-, 93
queries in URLs, 138–139
schema design and, 93–100
standards, 22
XML Schema and, 125, 126
SQL Queries for Mere Mortals: A Hands-On Guide to Data Manipulation in SQL (Hernandez), xiv
SQL Server (Microsoft)
basic description of, 129–158
Books Online, 136, 139
communicating with, over the Web, 134–136
DTDs and, 142
extensions, architecture of, 135–136
FOR XML AUTO clause, 132–133
FOR XML clause, 131–132, 136, 146, 147
FOR XML EXPLICIT clause, 133–134, 143
Query Analyzer, 134, 148
retrieving data in XML format and, 130–134, 136–144
schema and, 93

template files and, 138–141
working with XML documents and, 152–154
XML Views and, 141–146
SQLX, 127–128
Standards
basic description of, 23–24, 115–128
two types of, 24
startDocument method, 163
Stock quotes, 181–185
Storage issues, 17–18, 92
Stored procedures, 89
<strong> tag, 13, 14
SUBJECT element, 69, 70
Suggestions, science of, 109–113
Sun Microsystems, 23, 127, 147, 176
SVG (Scalable Vector Graphics), 24
Swatch, 78
Sweden, King of, 25–27, 45
Sybase, 93
Synchronization, 84, 99
Syntax rules, 65–66
System crashes, 68. *See also* Bugs; Errors

T

Tabs, 74. *See also* White space
Tags. *See also* Elements; Tags (listed by name)
hierarchical structure of, 13–14, 15
illegal, 85
opening/closing, pairs of, 77
Tags (listed by name). *See also* Tags
<b> tag, 70

 tag, 85
<document> tag, 8
<em> tag, 13, 14, 118–119
<i> tag, 70
<p> tag, 13, 85, 118–119
<strong> tag, 13, 14
<u> tag, 13
Tamura, Kent, 158
Tannenbaum, Andrew, 23
Taxonomical structure, 188–191
Technical specification document, 45–46
Template files, 138–141
Terseness, in XML markup, 17
Testers, training needs for, 40. *See also* Testing
Testing
integration, 39–52
plans, 39–40
priorities, 41
quality assurance and, 39
scenarios, 40
unit, 39
TEXT data type, 93
That's Not What I Meant: How Conversational Styles Makes or Breaks Relationships (Tannen), 35
TheStreet.com, x, 4
TIBCO, 125
Time
-boxed development, 42–43
brief history of, 77–78
DTD design and, 75, 77–78
-stamps, 75, 77, 197
zones, 77
TO element, 69
Transactions, 99

Index

Transformation mechanisms, 165–166, 171–172
Trees, 22–23, 94
Triggers, 89

U

UML (Unified Modeling Language), 35, 37–38, 54
Underlined font, 13
Unicode character set, 53
Unique IDs, 68, 94
Units of measure, 39
Unit testing, 39, 44–45
UNIX, 10, 120
UPDATE statement, 154
Uramoto, Naohiko, 158
URI (Uniform Resource Identifier), 83
URLs (Uniform Resource Locators), 79, 85–86. *See also* Links
    data modeling and, 55
    DTDs and, 80–81
    encoding, 137
    hard-coding documents with, 6
    parameters in, 139–140
    rewriting, 106
    sending templates in, 138–139
    specifying queries in, 139–141
    XLink and, 80
Use Case Driven Object Modeling with UML: A Practical Approach (Rosenberg and Scott), 38
Use cases, 37–38, 40, 54
User(s)
    entities, 54
    involvment, active, 42
    scenarios, 30–33
<u> tag, 13

V

Validation, 65–66
varchar data type, 53, 93
Vasa (battleship), 25–27, 42
VERSION attribute, 197
Versioning, 195–197
Virtual directories, 136, 137
Visual Basic (Microsoft), 148, 153
Visualization techniques, 54

W

W3C (World Wide Web Consortium), 12, 14–16, 111
    archive of DTDs, 86
    bandwidth issues and, 18
    basic description of, 24
    domain-specific languages and, 116
    XML Schema and, 125
    XML Views and, 142
    XPath and, 120
    XQuery and, 126–127
    XSL and, 121
WAP (Wireless Application Protocol), xviii, 4, 18, 24, 116
WebDav, 195
Web services, building, 180–185
WebSphere, 176
WHERE clause, 147
White space, 74, 85
Windows NT (Microsoft), 10
WITH statement, 154
WML (Wireless Markup Language), 4

Workflow states, 192–193

X
xCBL (XML Common Business Library), 86
XDR (XML Data-Reduced), 63, 121, 141–151
XHTML (eXtensible HTML), 84–85, 118, 119, 201
XLink (XML Linking Language), 79–82, 106, 111
XML: A Manager's Guide (Dick), xiv
XML and Java: Developing Web Applications (Maruyama, Tamura, and Uramoto), 158
XML Catalog, 86
XML.com, 86, 125–126
XMLDATA, 146, 148
XML.org, 86
XML Views, 141–151
XP (extreme programming), 43–45
XPath, 116, 119–120, 127, 141–144, 154
XQuery, 120, 126–127
XSL (eXtensible Style Language), 116
XSLT (eXtensible Stylesheet Language Transformation), 115–121, 165–166

Y
Y2K issues, 17

Z
ZIP compression format, 24

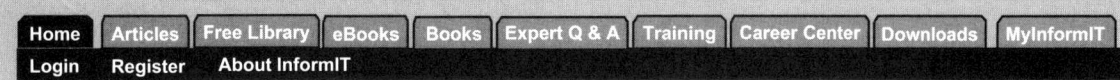

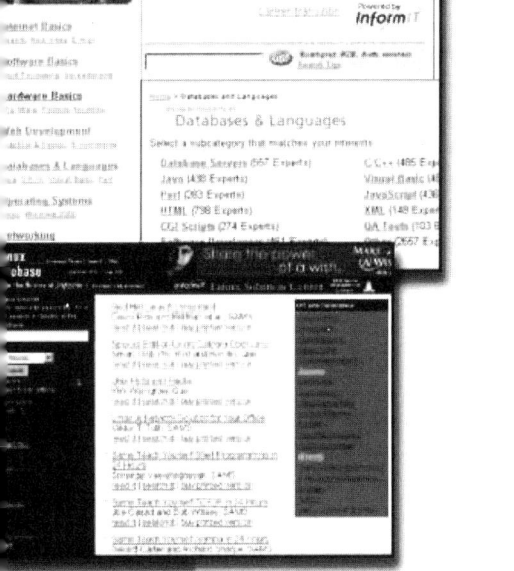

Register Your Book

at www.aw.com/cseng/register

You may be eligible to receive:
- Advance notice of forthcoming editions of the book
- Related book recommendations
- Chapter excerpts and supplements of forthcoming titles
- Information about special contests and promotions throughout the year
- Notices and reminders about author appearances, tradeshows, and online chats with special guests

Contact us

If you are interested in writing a book or reviewing manuscripts prior to publication, please write to us at:

Editorial Department
Addison-Wesley Professional
75 Arlington Street, Suite 300
Boston, MA 02116 USA
Email: AWPro@aw.com

Visit us on the Web: http://www.aw.com/cseng